Fabrics for Embroidery

Fabrics for Embroidery

Jean Littlejohn

Photographs by Dudley Moss

B.T. Batsford Ltd LONDON

Acknowledgements

I have always been most fortunate in having support and encouragement from all the people around me.

My parents, husband Philip and daughter Hannah give practical help, moral support and friendly criticism.

The embroidery students at Windsor and Maidenhead College of Further Education are very generous with their work and I owe them many thanks for allowing it to be photographed by Dudley Moss, who takes great trouble to do justice to the pieces.

My greatest thanks must go to my friend and colleague Jan Beaney, who first introduced me to embroidery, fostered my interest, expanded my horizons and continues to provide inspiration.

JEAN LITTLEJOHN
Maidenhead 1986

© Jean Littlejohn 1986
First published 1986

ISBN 0 7134 5112 2

Typeset by Servis Filmsetting Ltd,
Manchester
and printed in Great Britain by
The Bath Press
Bath
for the publishers
B.T. Batsford Ltd
4 Fitzhardinge Street
London W1H 0AH

Embroideries are by the author unless otherwise credited.

Contents

Introduction

Fabrics have surfaces and properties which allow them to be stitched in countless ways. These qualities have been appreciated over centuries by people who have taken pride and pleasure in handling and working with them.

The modern embroiderer is confronted with a vast array of exciting fabrics from which to choose. Such unlimited choice can sometimes lead to indecision and pose further problems for the designer.

In times when fabrics were not so plentiful or varied, embroiderers were compelled to exercise great ingenuity in order to create new designs. It is thought that decorating fabric with a needle dates back as far as 3000 BC. Because fabrics are vulnerable to the ravages of time, few ancient embroideries have survived apart from those preserved in special conditions such as tombs.

In Siberia, frozen tombs from the fifth century BC, excavated when the ground thawed, yielded intricate leather and felt appliqué showing a high level of skill and design. Other tombs in South America, China, India and Egypt have also revealed the skills of the ancient embroiderer, and indicate how much has perished over the centuries.

Before extensive world trade in the sixteenth and seventeenth centuries enabled new fabrics to pass from one country to another, embroiderers were limited to those in their immediate environment. These limitations encouraged people to be endlessly inventive with the materials at their disposal.

Across Europe, linen has been obtained from flax for centuries. The structured nature of the weaves encouraged counted thread, pulled and drawn work. But despite the geometric nature of such techniques, numerous variations and textures have been achieved. Colours were dictated by local plant dyes, and patterns influenced by the environment and cultural background (see figs 1–5).

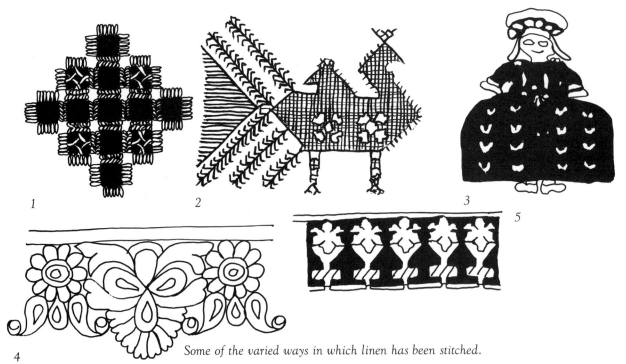

Some of the varied ways in which linen has been stitched.

1 *Hardanger cut work from Norway: linen thread on a linen ground.*

2 *Bird motif from Finland, worked in linen on a linen ground.*

3 *Greek island (Janina) motif from a long cushion: silk on linen using double running stitch.*

4 *Detail from a Czechoslovakian costume: satin stitch using wool on linen.*

5 *Seventeenth-century embroidered band from Spain, in silk on linen.*

When European settlers first arrived in North America they found a dearth of fabrics – no sheep for wool, no flax for linen and no suitable cotton. Until they started to produce their own fabrics, all their ingenuity was diverted into embroideries which conserved precious fabrics and threads. The work carried out usually reflected the country of origin, but was worked smaller or less richly. A surface satin stitch was used to economize on threads. In the 1770s patchwork developed as an excellent way of conserving and re-using much-valued fabrics. Thus the potential drawback of scarce fabrics was developed into a great strength of American embroidery, where patchwork has become an art form.

Other physical factors have also influenced the development of fabrics for embroidery. Cold climates encouraged work which added much-needed warmth. Very heavy surface stitching, quilting and the use of thick fabrics and animal skins was carried out extensively in parts of northern Europe and North America. In Hungary, leather and felt appliqué has long been carried out, usually by men (figs 6, 7).

8

6,7 *Two motifs from Hungary;* **6** *leather on felt;* **7** *the back panel from a leather appliqué jacket; both pieces worked by men.*

Some cultures have been highly inventive in using specialized local materials. Groups of North American Indians have used softened birchbark as a ground material. In Alaska, Aleuts and other Eskimo groups worked on fish skins and the dried intestines of seals. Shells have been incorporated in designs in Africa, and in India metallic-looking beetles' wings have been used to decorate embroideries. Quills obtained from porcupines and birds, chewed and softened, have been widely used by North American Indians. In the search to expand the range of materials, the headhunters of South America were even known to use human hair in their weavings and embroideries.

Sericulture (silk farming) was first discovered in China about 2000 BC and strongly influenced Chinese designs. Fine lustre fabrics and threads were worked in rich and delicate motifs (figs 8, 9). After the sixth century AD silk spread gradually through Asia and into Europe, and consequently influenced the designs worked there.

9 *Nineteeth-century Chinese sleeveband, a voided butterfly in silk satin stitch on silk.*

8 *Japanese voided chrysanthemum, silk satin stitch on a silk ground.*

It is interesting to note that embroidery has often been considered inferior to the skills of weaving and used as a cheaper imitation of another technique. Damask darning simulates damask weaving, and Carrick-macross (a form of net appliqué) was designed as an imitation of Brussels and guipure laces. They are now both recognized for their own qualities.

The richness and type of embroidery is dictated largely by the fabrics available, and we are fortunate nowadays in having an enormous variety from which to select. This may be looked upon as an exciting opportunity, providing the embroiderer develops a sensitivity to the special qualities of each fabric and uses them appropriately.

One approach towards work with fabrics is to have in mind a design and search out the right fabric. This is not always easy, despite the choice, as a fabric of the correct colour may have an unsuitable texture or handling property. Some people are so excited by a piece of fabric, however, that they determine to use it and work at suitable designs.

Notebooks and sketchbooks are much more useful if they contain snippets of fabric for future reference. A great deal of time can be lost rummaging through scrap bags in a vain attempt to trace a fabric you remember, only to discover that it isn't quite the right colour. Take small samples of fabrics as you acquire them and stick them in a notebook, perhaps with some ideas of how they might be used (see fig. 10). The most successful results are achieved by marrying a good design to suitable fabrics and threads.

Synthetic fabrics and threads are easily available and have been developed for their wash-and-wear qualities and colourfastness. It is these qualities, however, which make them difficult to manipulate into soft gentle folds, as their resilience resists this. Traditional fabrics which accept handling and stay in contorted shapes without springing back are often more suitable.

10 *Page from a notebook with sketches, cut paper designs and fabric samples indicating possible interpretations.*

10

Any fabric which has an obvious texture or pattern may be too obtrusive for a sensitive design, and distract the viewer from the intended focal point.

Fine stitching may look wrong on coarse fabrics, or wool on silk, although there are of course exceptions where discord is intended. Despite the range of fabrics available, some designers are extending the boundaries of embroidery by constructing their own fabrics or incorporating wood, wire, paper etc. in their work.

In this book, I am looking at particular groups of fabrics with specific properties and considering ways of using them. It is not intended to be a comprehensive technique book, as there are many excellent ones available.

Included in the illustrations are pages from sample notebooks which are designed to whet the appetite for further experiments rather than to provide all the answers. It is exciting to discover new ways of using fabrics, and it would be a shame to pre-empt that.

Basic instructions for many of the techniques are indicated and there is a bibliography detailing books which will provide further information.

Fabrics are a pleasure to handle, and embroideries where they have been used sensitively, a joy to behold.

11 *'Wall Texture'. The bubbly effect was achieved by holding the fabric over a candle flame (not touching), and allowing it to melt and distort the fibres. Further texture has been added by fraying, folding, ruching, plaiting, etc. (Ann Sutton)*

ONE
Fabric manipulation

Fabric manipulation simply means methods of organizing and stitching fabrics into a design. This may be a free textured surface or a formal regulated pattern. The success of the work depends greatly on the type of fabric used. Some embroideries have areas of applied fabrics which sit awkwardly on a background with little attempt to integrate them.

As an introduction to fabric manipulation, select a piece of soft cotton or calico and work a small sampler. Frame a piece of fabric to use as a background and use other pieces of the same fabric to see how many textures may be achieved. Pin them into position and stitch down to secure, using a thread of a matching colour. By using the same fabric and matching thread there will be no colour or texture contrast to detract from the simplicity of the exercise (see fig. 12).

The numerous possibilities include:

- torn strips;
- gathering;
- fraying;
- folding;
- pleating;
- tucking;
- rolls of fabric;
- twists and curls;
- ruching;
- plaiting;
- rouleaus;
- cords and braids.

Experiments using a wide variety of fabrics will build up extensive knowledge of how fabrics handle, and will be of great benefit when working further embroideries.

Having discovered some interesting textures, progress to a simple design based on perhaps a landscape or a natural form. Select from the textures you have discovered to carry out the design, always bearing in mind that this is a fabric interpretation and not to be too literal. Using just one fabric sharpens the sense of texture and throws up cast shadows on to the piece of work. When satisfied with the arrangement of the pieces, stitch them into place with small stab stitches, using a matching thread.

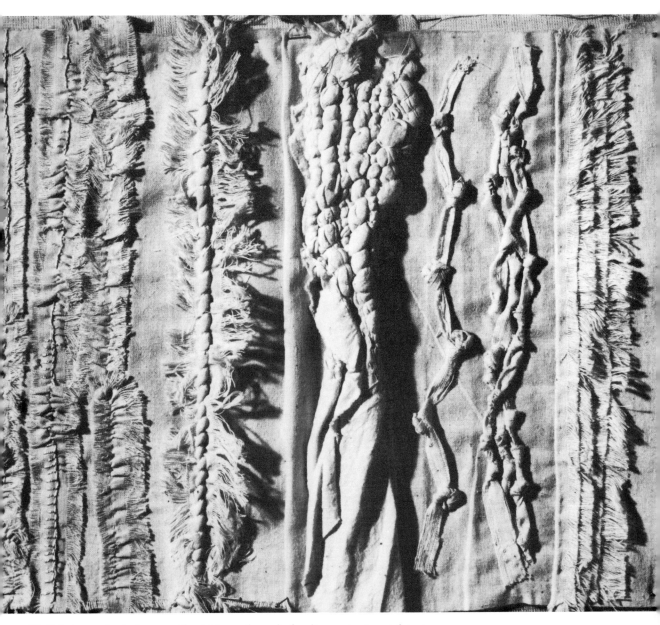

12 *Fabric manipulation sample. Using soft washed calico, experimental textures have been achieved by folding, twisting, knotting and fraying. (Shirley Warren)*

15

Fabrics which fray

Most fabrics fray to some extent, and a frayed edge can be attractive in some pieces of work. There are several ways of treating fabrics with fraying edges which can be used according to the design.

Turned edge
A simple turning using small overcasting or slip stitches in a matching thread.

Frayed edge
The edge is held down with tiny stitches in a matching thread. Where an article is subject to wear and tear, a stronger method such as machine stitching or back stitch should be used.

Burned edge
Some fabrics such as cotton may be singed near a candle flame to prevent fraying. When the edge has the desired shape, snuff the smouldering edge with dampened fingers, and always have available a bowl of water and a fire-resistant surface. Some synthetic fibres will flare dangerously, so take great care. This method seals the edge.

Sealed edge
PVA glues may be used to prevent frayed edges. The glue should be applied sparingly with a fine implement such as a cocktail stick and it will dry transparent, although stiff. Rubber-based adhesives eventually turn yellow and spoil the effect of the fabric.

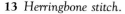

13 *Herringbone stitch.*

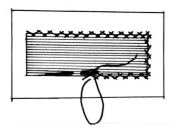

Herringbone stitch
This stitch is often used when applying a fraying fabric to a background, using a strong thread in a matching colour as unobtrusively as possible (fig. 13).

Machine appliqué
Apply fabrics to a background using the zig-zag stitch on a sewing machine. The stitch may vary from satin stitch to open zig-zag – this will be dictated by the design (fig. 14).

Net
Pieces of frayable fabric may be held in place by net or other semi-transparent fabric, where the design allows (fig. 15).

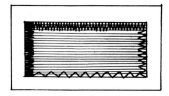

14 *Machine zig-zag varying from open to closed.*

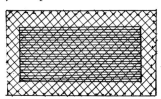

15 *Net applied over a piece of fabric to a ground.*

16 *Haphazard appliqué.*

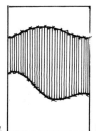 

a *b* *c*

17 *Appliqué, with indications of how stitching could be used to blend it with the background fabric.*

Haphazard appliqué
Pieces of fabric are splattered over the background and machined over with zig-zag, to be absorbed in the design (fig. 16).

Stitching
The use of stitches such as seeding can blend a fabric into the background where a hard edge is not wanted. Cretan stitch, straight stitch and many others may be used to marry a fabric into a design (fig. 17).

Iron-on interfacing
When a fabric is ironed on to dressmakers' interfacing, excess fraying is prevented, although the edge can crumble if overworked. This can alter the surface and quality of the fabric, and there are cases where it could be unsuitable.

Raised and textured surfaces

Trapunto (isolated quilted areas)
Two layers are necessary. Add a piece of fabric to the surface of the design, or behind the required area. Stitch around the edge of the shape to be padded, through the two layers, using back stitch, running stitch or machine stitching (fig. 18a). On the wrong side of the fabric, slash the background and stuff with kapok or other padding. Overcast the slit and this will result in a raised area on the front of the design (fig. 18b).

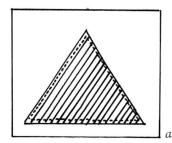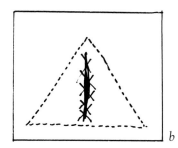

18 *Trapunto*

Padded patches
1 Apply a fabric shape to a background, usually with a small turned edge. (If working in leather or felt, the turned edge is not necessary.) Stitch around the edge of the shape with small overcasting stitches in a matching thread, leaving a small opening through which to ease the stuffing. Close the opening when the stuffing is sufficient (fig. 19).
2 A raised shape can be built up with felt contours. A final piece is laid over the top and stitched in place (fig. 20).

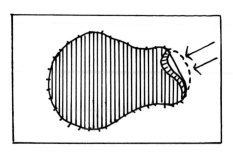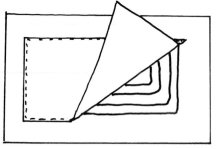

19 *Padded patch.*

20 *Felt contours, padded patch.*

Raised ball-like shapes
Take a small blob of kapok or other stuffing. Place it on a circular piece of a stretchy fabric such as tights, muslin or scrim (fig. 21a). Enclose the stuffing in the fabric and secure by stitching or binding the loose edges (figs 21b, c). These shapes may be large or small, and a combination of the two looks effective with other textures (fig. 21d).

21 *The stages necessary to make raised padded balls, with a design suggestion.*

Ruching
Pin the ruched areas of fabric on to the background, taking care to avoid giving them the appearance of being 'plonked' on the surface.

By using a soft, easily manipulated fabric such as muslin and blending it into the background with stitching, unsympathetic shapes can be avoided.

Very springy synthetic fibres are more difficult to work in this technique.

Moulding
Some fabrics with a dressing may be moulded when damp into simple shapes. Scrims and hessians can be used in this way.

After damping the fabric, pin out on polystyrene or pinboard into ridges or bumps and allow to dry. It is also possible to mould over simple shapes like bottle tops. When dry, these shapes may be applied to embroideries and blended in with stitches.

Moulding with glue

Sometimes you may need to apply a rigid shape to a design. Absorbent fabrics may be saturated with wallpaper paste or PVA glue, moulded into shapes, and when dry applied to a background.

Although lending stiffness, these techniques retain a quality of surface which is special to fabrics.

Moulding with plaster of Paris

Fabric dipped in a weak solution of plaster of Paris also moulds into shapes which may be applied or stitched. Careful thought should be given to the fabric qualities of this technique and to how much rigidity is acceptable.

Rouleaus

Cut a strip of fabric on the bias. Fold in half lengthways and machine along the wrong side, leaving a small turning (figs 22a, b). Turn it out to the right side (fig. 22c).

The rouleau may be applied as a cord, and if a more rigid shape is necessary, wool or cord may be inserted (fig. 22e).

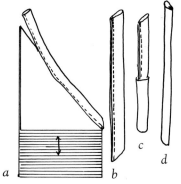

22 *The stages in making a rouleau, with a design suggestion.*

Tucks and ridges

Make a fold in the fabric and stitch along the edge to the required depth of the tuck. The stitching may be worked by machine or hand. Groups of tucks and ridges of varying sizes look well together and they may be stuffed and slashed to vary the effect (fig. 23).

23 *Tucks and ridges.*

Pleats
Fold the fabric into even or uneven groups and hold in place by machine or hand stitching. Pleats have a flatter appearance than tucks and ridges, but can be used as a contrast.

Gathering
Using a strong thread with a knot, work running stitches along the length of the fabric to be gathered, pull up and secure. The resulting piece of fabric may then be applied as with ruching.

Loosely woven fabrics such as muslin and scrim gather in interesting ways when a thread is pulled in the fabric and secured in place.

Smocking
Smocking is an organized system of controlling fullness by means of gathers. Although normally used for clothes, it may successfully be incorporated in free embroidery.

There are many ways in which it is possible to experiment with smocking, including the following:

1 Pull up the gathers in the usual way and work decorative smocking stitches on the surface as the design requires. For this it is not necessary to work the stitches evenly or in straight rows.
2 Pull up the gathers in the usual way and on the back work honeycomb in a matching thread so that it does not show on the front. Remove the gathering threads and the right side will consist of flexible empty gathers on which to stitch in a variety of ways.

The smocking may be applied to a background and further stitching worked.

Slashing
Slash the surface of a fabric either in selected areas or at random and draw
fabrics through the slashes (fig. 24).

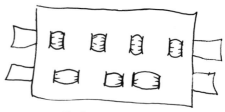

24 *Slashing.*

Stretching over card
Stretch fabric over a card shape, which may be padded, according to the
effect desired. Lace the fabric over the back of the card with strong thread
(fig. 25a). This gives a crisp form which may contrast well with textured
areas.

Stitch to the background fabric with overcasting in a matching thread.

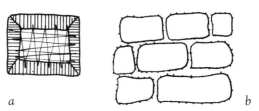

a   *b*

25 *Stretching fabric over card, with a
design idea.*

Quilting
Quilting is a technique where layers of fabric are held together with
stitching and cast shadows over the surface of the fabric. It is a subtle
technique, and should not be forgotten when considering ways of varying
fabric surfaces. There are many excellent books detailing the techniques
of:

- English wadded quilting;
- Italian quilting;
- tied quilting;
- corded quilting.

26 *Three fabric samples worked on fine silk: a English and tied quilting; b padded patches, trapunto, covered card shapes and applied squares; c strips of texture by tucking, folding, ruching, balls of fabric, Italian quilting, rouleaus and burned edges.*

27 'Flying Bug'. A variety of fabric manipulation techniques have been combined to create the bug. Burned synthetic organzas overlapping with free machine embroidery have been stretched over a wire frame. (Karen Hall)

28 'Irises'. Transfer dyes have been used to print the design on to a fabric which was then stitched with a twin needle, slashed, frayed and applied to a ground fabric. (Georgina Rees)

29,30 '*Wall Textures*'. *The richly encrusted surface combines ridges, tucks, machine pulled work, ruching, fraying and surface stitching in a variety of fabrics.* (Ann Sutton)

27

31 *Fabric manipulation sample. The ball-like shapes have been covered in stockinette and nylon tights, and enclosed in a structure of freely folded linen. (June James)*

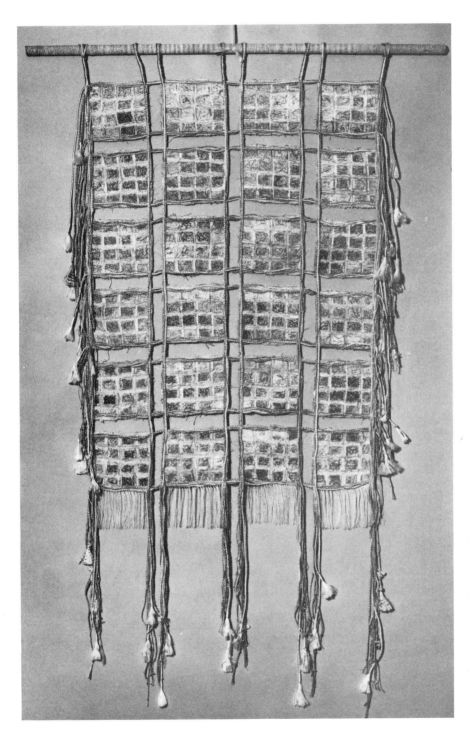

32 'Grids'. The background is a furnishing fabric with a loose weave. The surface was machine embroidered with metallic and other threads. Further pieces of fabric were applied over the top and cut away, the frayed edges revealing squares of texture underneath. The cords which hold the pieces in place have been whipped with machine zig-zag. (Mavis Graham)

33 *'Bent Tin'. The tin has been constructed from pre-dyed calico and stiffened with glue before being moulded into a crumpled shape. (Ann Marchbanks)*

34 *'Dried Hydrangea'. Linen scrim, dampened and moulded, forms the basis of this delicate piece, with pre-dyed scrim petals added afterwards on a covered wire stem. (Diana Spencer)*

FACING PAGE
35 *'Notice Board'. With the exception of the poster and newspaper cutting, all the other items on the notice board have been made from fabrics treated in a variety of ways. The computer paper has been made from dyed cotton, stiffened in wallpaper paste. Other techniques used include machine embroidery, dyeing and appliqué. (Karen Hall)*

me in the Jungle

hen home embroidery is far
more stimulating than men . . .

Shopping

Nappies
Bread
Edam - other cheese
Jiff   Bank
Persil auto
fish
Saladstuff

at Windsor and Maidenhead College of F.E.
The Annexe. Osborne Rd. Windsor. Tel. No 64745
on
Wed 19th, Thurs 20th, Fri 21st June 10am-9pm

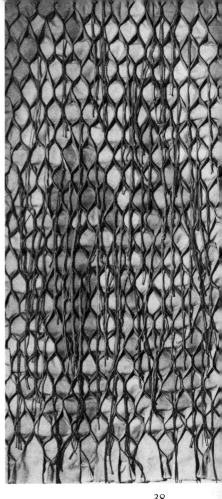

38

37

36 'Cockerel'. On a frame of wire, padded shapes have been used as a base. The fabrics include synthetic organzas, lining materials and a variety of yarns. The feathers, individually made, have been clipped, torn and frayed, and the comb made using solid cable stitch on the machine. (Pam Parker)

37 'In and Out of Focus'. Gathering stitches used to draw up the smocking gathers have been left in place to create this flexible piece of work. The figures were printed on to the fabric after the gathers were tightly drawn together. When opened out, interesting spaces were left between the gathers. (June Linsley)

38 'Rose Trellis'. On to a piece of pre-dyed calico, calico shapes were applied. Vertical tucks were then machined into the fabric, and these have been used as a basis for honeycomb smocking. Further threads have been added to create the foliage. (Phyllis Gunstone)

39 *'Wall'. A variety of fabrics have been manipulated on a calico ground. Cotton, silk and chiffon have been dyed, ridged, frayed, slashed and ruched to create the strata. Leather strips and surface stitches have been added to complete the effect.* (Georgina Rees)

40 *'Fireplace'. A variety of techniques have been combined to make this fireplace. The wood surround has been achieved by stretching moiré taffeta over card. The black 'leading' hood has been made with trapunto and corded quilting. The tiles, made from silk and painted with silk dyes, were patchworked together. The logs in the grate have been manipulated in hessian. The lace mantel cloth, based on a William Morris style, was machined on spun alginate fabric and dissolved to form the lace. (Georgina Grant)*

35

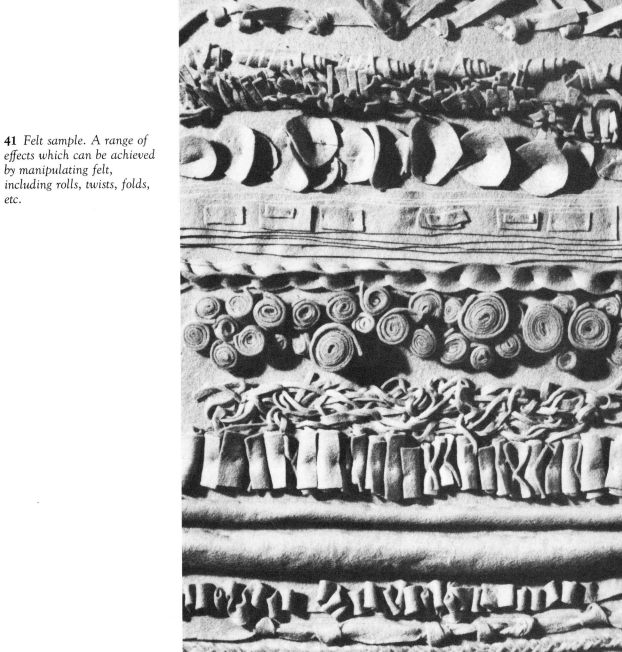

41 *Felt sample. A range of effects which can be achieved by manipulating felt, including rolls, twists, folds, etc.*

42 *Two felt bags worked in appliqué.* (Mary Shea)

Non-fraying fabrics

Felt and leather are fabrics which have a long historical tradition. They have the special advantage of non-fraying edges.

Felt
A non-woven material formed by the compression of woollen fibres, felt has been widely used in embroidery because it is easy to cut and stitch.

It has many more possibilities than the straight appliqué for which it has so often been used. It may be twisted and manipulated in an endless variety of ways which catch the light and produce exciting sculptural effects. The applied pieces may be stitched with tiny stab stitches close to the edge, taking care not to crumble the fabric. The stitches should not be pulled too tightly, as this detracts from the smooth appearance of the design. Further possibilities with felt can be achieved by cutting through it to reveal layers below. Other fabrics may be used as a contrast between the layers.

43 *Felt samples. Samples of felt layers sandwiching contrasting fabrics. After surface machining, the layers have been cut through using very sharp scissors, to reveal the layers underneath. (Jenni Last)*

44,45 *Two felt pieces. The collar comprises two layers of felt which have been machined together and the top cut through to reveal the lighter-coloured felt underneath. The jacket has been sprayed and quilted with felt floral shapes applied to the surface to add another dimension. (Diana Seidl)*

38

Leather
Leather may be used in similar ways to felt, although it is more difficult to sew and handle. For ease of sewing, select soft glove leathers. Because it has both smooth and rough surfaces leather can be most useful in textured panels. The edges of some skins have a tatty and bedraggled appearance which can be incorporated successfully in embroideries. Leather may be stitched with small stab stitches using a strong thread. It will mark if pinned into position, so it is better to hold shapes in place before final stitching with long holding stitches.

Gold and silver kid have been used extensively in metal thread work as a contrasting texture and may be padded because of the stretchy quality of the leather.

FACING PAGE
46 *'Wall'. Leather scraps applied to a calico ground, including the rough and smooth sides of the leather and some ragged edges.* (Tess Marsh)

47 *'Wall'. Pre-dyed leather shapes have been applied to a calico ground, with net scrim and surface stitching added to create the impression of a flint wall.* (Audrey King)

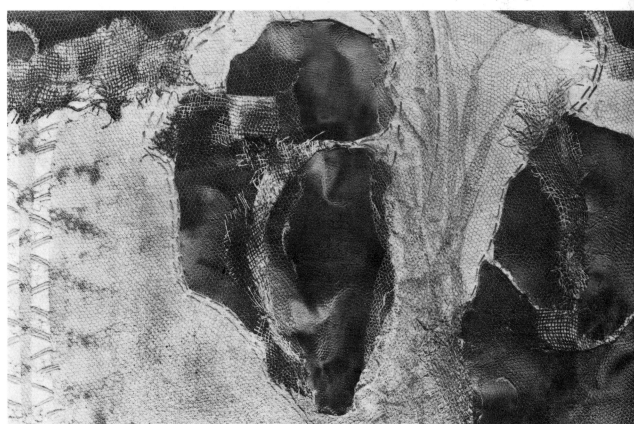

TWO

Transparent and sheer fabrics

Sheer fabrics have a special delicate quality of lightness and fragility which can be used successfully in embroidery. They include organdie, organza, net, jap silk, georgette, voile and even plastic. They differ widely in their handling properties but can add atmosphere to designs.

They may be used in layers rather like watercolour paint. This will result in subtle and unusual colour combinations.

Depending on type, they may fray or tear easily or pull into holes. For functional household articles, synthetic and man-made fibres which wash well may be more suitable, but the softer more compliant natural fibres are a great pleasure to handle and to embroider.

Considerations when using sheer fabrics

Stitching
Stitching can often show through from the back to the front, so careful planning is needed to avoid unwanted shadowy patterns showing through.

Threads
As with most embroideries, the threads should reflect the type of fabric used, so silk on silk or cotton on cotton, etc., are usually the most effective. There are of course exceptions to this, depending on the design.

Dyes
Most transparent fabrics may be dyed, but they have a less solid image than an opaque fabric, which can be an advantage.

Framing
Special consideration should be given to display of transparent work before the embroidery is undertaken, as heavy unsympathetic mounting might destroy the illusion created by the delicate work.

48 *Shadow quilting sample. A variety of threads, ribbons, lace and beads have been stitched between two layers of organdie to create subtle shadows through the fabric.*

43

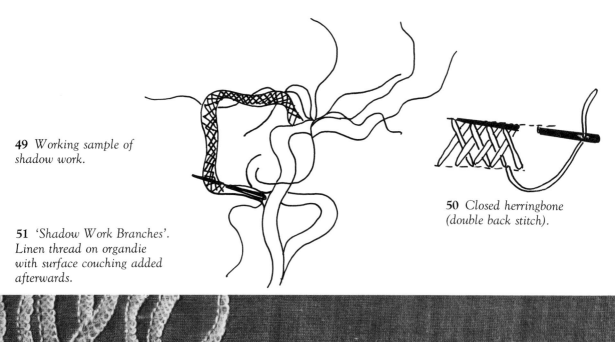

49 *Working sample of shadow work.*

50 *Closed herringbone (double back stitch).*

51 *'Shadow Work Branches'. Linen thread on organdie with surface couching added afterwards.*

Transparent fabrics have featured strongly in traditional British and foreign embroidery. Techniques exploiting these fabrics include:

- shadow work;
- shadow quilting;
- Carrickmacross;
- net appliqué.

Developing from their traditional use, there is a great deal of scope for modern interpretations.

Shadow work

A technique popular in the eighteenth century, shadow work consists of stitching worked on the reverse of the fabric which shows through as a shadowy image on the front. It is traditionally worked in white threads on a white ground, although some modern pieces have featured colour with varying degrees of success.

Design
The design should be broken down into pairs of lines not necessarily parallel but preferably no further than 12 mm apart. Floral flowing lines have been widely used in the past.

Transfer of design
The design can be drawn on to thick paper. It should then be pinned or tacked to the fabric, wrong side uppermost. Trace the design on to the fabric using a fine white watercolour line or with a white pencil.

Method
On the wrong side of the fabric work a close herringbone (double back) stitch (fig. 50). On the front this will look like two rows of back stitch, with the shadow of herringbone stitch showing through – hence the name.

To develop this technique, further stitching may be added to the surface and combined with dyes and coloured threads, always bearing in mind the delicacy of the technique.

Shadow quilting

Shadow quilting consists of two layers of sheer fabric held together by stitching, entrapping coloured threads and fabrics between them. It is a most exciting form of embroidery which has become more widespread. All manner of textures and fibres may be used, and will have a special quality because the transparent surface will subtly alter the colour.

Design
A wide variety of designs may be interpreted in this technique, from pure pattern to natural forms. Draw the design on to paper with a waterproof felt pen so that it may be seen through the fabric.

Method
Iron the two pieces of fabric, as wrinkles are difficult to straighten out when stitching has been completed. Place the backing fabric, wrong side uppermost, over the design. Arrange the central pieces of fabric or thread on the background. Place the top layer over the work, surface uppermost, and tack through all the pieces so that they will not move during stitching. In a fragmented design, a tiny spot of PVA glue may be used under the central pieces to hold them in place.

Stitching
Stab stitch, back stitch or machine stitch where necessary to hold the layers in place. It has been conventional to leave spaces between the shapes, but as with most techniques, breaking the rules has led to exciting effects. Overlapping, the use of dyes and combinations of surface stitching and appliqué make this one of the most exciting techniques available to the embroiderer.

Variations of this technique include Italian shadow quilting, where channels of stitching through the two layers of fabric are threaded with ribbons, etc., and stuffed shadow quilting (trapunto), where the under fabric is slashed, and stuffing or beads are trapped in shapes sewn in the transparent fabric (see fig. 48).

52 *'Great Auntie Esther'. Transfer dyes have been used to print the image on to organdie. Scraps of fabric, including net, have been sandwiched between the layers, and surface stitching holds the layers in place and adds decoration. (Jan Beaney)*

53 *Shadow quilting sample. A combination of dyes, newspaper cuttings and surface stitching has been used in this sample* (Shirley Warren)

54 *'Shadow Work Apples'. The apple motif has been printed on to the organdie with transfer dyes and combined with machine embroidery to form the pattern.* (Karen Hall)

55 'My Fair Lady'. *Synthetic organza encloses a variety of fabrics to give the impression of images from the musical* My Fair Lady. *Surface stitching and couched ribbons have been added to complete the piece.* (Janet Wilcox)

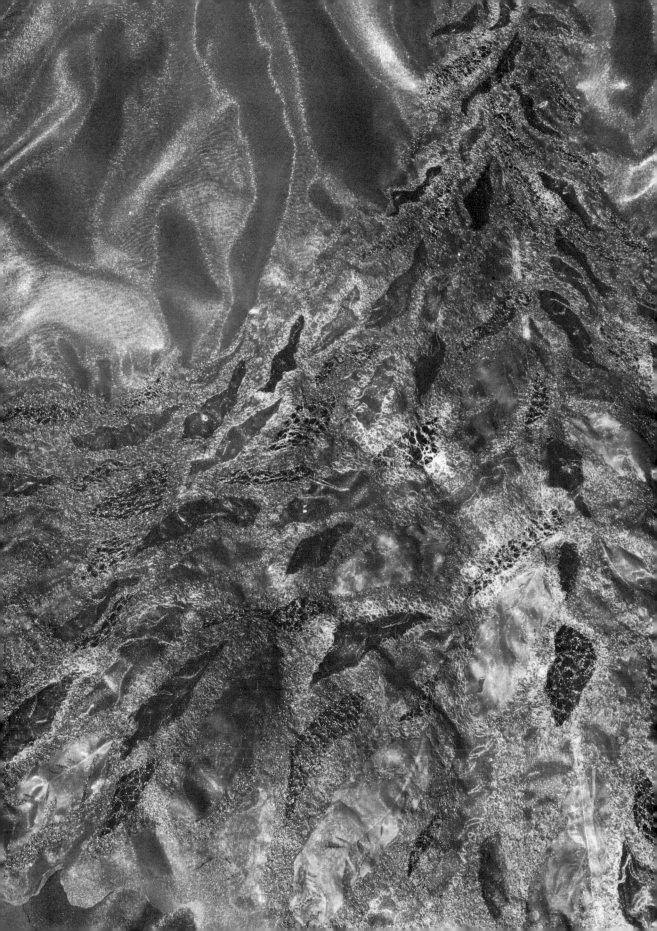

FACING PAGE
56 *Part of an evening cloak. Synthetic crystal organza has been used in layers, enclosing feathers and fabric shapes with surface machine embroidery.* (Gail Harker)

57 *'Clematis'. On layers of fine cotton voile, dyes have been used in combination with net, cotton and silk applied shapes to create the feeling of depth with sensitivity. Surface seeding and running stitch have added texture and definition to parts of the panel.* (Pam Parker)

58 *Carrickmacross sample.*
The dyed cotton flowers and
frame were applied to the net
ground as a complete piece.
After machining, the excess
background was trimmed
away to reveal the net
underneath. (Roy Hirst)

59 *Net sample. Irregular-shaped pieces of fabric have been freely machined to a*
ground of synthetic net. (Rosemary Jarvis)

Carrickmacross and net appliqué

Carrickmacross is a simulated lace developed in Ireland in the nineteenth century. The net ground is decorated with applied closely woven muslin shapes, usually white on white and outlined with couching. Drawn fabric stitches are sometimes used to complete the design.

Method
A fine muslin or other suitable fabric is placed over the net. Stitch the main outlines of the design through both layers with a linen thread, couched closely with a fine thread. Trim the excess surface fabric away from the shapes. Add further surface stitching if necessary.

Working with beautiful colours and synthetic fibres, this little-used technique has much potential. Hand or machine embroidery may be used to hold the shapes in place for a less rigid appearance. For purely decorative purposes, different weights and qualities of fabric can be combined. Beads and ribbons can add texture to the surface, always remembering not to destroy the delicate nature of the technique. Dyes used on the net ground or on the applied fabrics offer further possibilities.

60 *Carrickmacross motif from a fichu of c.1840, muslin on cotton net.*

61 'Cabaret (Each and every one a virgin!)'. *The figures of the dancers from the musical Cabaret have been machined and hand stitched to the surface and underside of the net ground. Beads and yarns have been added to create a deliberately seedy effect. The net has been draped over layers of chiffon and rayon ironed on to a hessian ground.* (Judith Smalley)

62 'Frosty Window'. *The window, which is a box which opens, contains a stitched and dyed landscape viewed through net window panes with applied glitter and stitching.* (Diana Seidl)

54

63 *A few of the many weaves and open fabrics available.*

a

b

77 *Traditional filet darning motifs from table mats.*

Filet or lacis darning

Filet darning is a simple form of lace which consists of pattern darning on a square mesh net. This type of darning has a characteristic appearance dictated by the special net used.

Originally filet darning was worked on a hand-knotted square net. Although rare, hand-knotted nets are still available, but there are several synthetic machine-made nets which can be used, though they look and handle differently. It is also possible to construct a home-made knotted net.

Traditional approach
Darning has been most frequently worked in white or cream thread on white or cream net.

Design
It is geometric in nature because of the square net. Small isolated areas are best avoided, and the outline shapes should be carefully considered to prevent the formation of dull, solid blocks. Where large shapes occur, consider unworked areas within the shapes. Simple repeat patterns look good in this technique.

Transfer the design to graph paper, preferably of the same scale as the fabric to ensure success.

Method
A frame is essential to keep the vertical and horizontal threads firmly placed. There are special frames for this technique, but simple square wooden frames may be used. Pull the fabric taut, but leave just enough play for the needle to be darned in and out. Work the stitches on the net using a sympathetic thread and a blunt-ended needle.

68

76 *'Norfolk Landscape'. Surface darning using a variety of threads. (Mary Tasker)*

Surface darning

Traditional approach
This is the technique used for mending and strengthening fabrics – socks, for instance. When using a matching thread, holes may be repaired with an almost invisible new fabric. When worked decoratively in contrasting threads, new areas of design may be added and blended into the background.

Method
Work a structure of horizontal or vertical threads on the surface of the fabric, taking them further than the edge to prevent further damage to the hole. Darn the laid threads over and under alternatively, filling the shape and securing into the fabric at either side (fig. 74).

This method may be used to add a further surface to fabrics and combined with other forms of darning to create different levels. Some of the laid threads may be left unworked to enhance a particular design.

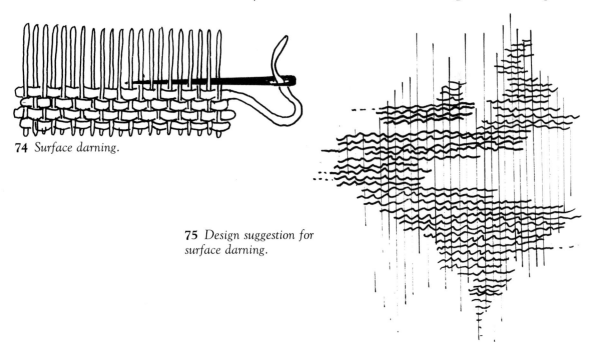

74 *Surface darning.*

75 *Design suggestion for surface darning.*

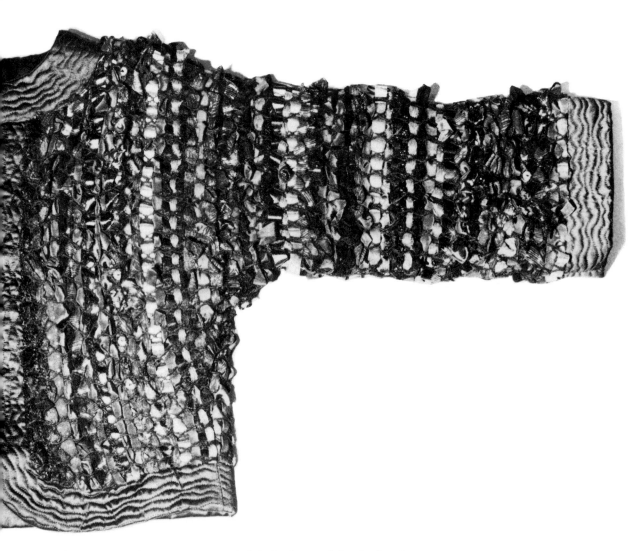

73 *Jacket. Large-mesh curtain net provided the background for the free darning worked in torn strips of fabric and ribbons. The edges have been finished with English quilting on satin.* (Rosemary Jarvis)

72 *'Wall Texture'. Using a vegetable bag as a base, torn fabrics, chenilles and other threads have been freely darned. (Ann Sutton)*

Free darning

As with most techniques, there are limitless possibilities using traditional fabrics and threads but combining them with modern materials such as curtain nets, plastic vegetable bags and even fabric strips and threads. Variations can be:

- a less formal approach to the pattern of stitches;
- variation in length of stitch;
- variation in direction of stitches;
- contrasts of shiny and matt surfaces;
- the building up of several layers of stitches.

71 *Darning sample. On to a large meshed plastic garden net, vegetable-dyed yarns were darned vertically and horizontally to build up a rich texture.* (Shirley Warren)

'Seascape'. Openweave
ol has been freely darned
a variety of yarns to
te a subtle seascape. The
chairs and people were
ked in silk on net and
lied to the background.
il Palmer)

Detail of the seascape in
69.

67 *'Landscape'. Dyes have been sponged on to a linen ground and pattern darning worked freely to create a sensitive landscape. (Ros Chilcot)*

Pattern darning

Traditional approach
This may be used as a background or for the motif. Straight stitches are arranged to form an endless variety of patterns, all over or in groups. The stitch length and the amount of ground covered may be varied to create new patterns.

Fabric and threads
An evenweave fabric is needed, with a compatible thread of the same weight and quality, using a tapestry needle.

Coloured threads have been used to good effect, but a very subtle surface is created when self-coloured threads are used.

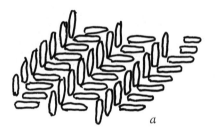
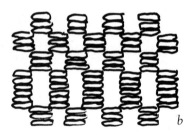

a b

68 *Two possible pattern darning combinations.*

Free pattern darning

Variety may be added to this technique by:

● the use of dyed background fabric;
● varying the type of background fabric or perhaps combining more than one type;
● varying the thickness and type of thread;
● stitches used in irregular designs.

Darning

Darning has a considerable history as a form of surface decoration or for mending holes in cloth. It does have a dull image which is quite unjustified as it is one of the most exciting and versatile techniques available to the embroiderer. Darning can be worked in and amongst the fibres of the ground material to enrich and enhance the surface so that it is very sympathetic to the fabric. Darning has been worked on linens, heavy cottons, wool and silk, but now people are experimenting successfully with household materials such as curtain nets and even plastic vegetable bags.

In its simplest form darning consists of straight stitches taken over the surface of the fabric, picking up a thread or two of the fabric between each one. It can be roughly broken down into:

- pattern darning;
- surface darning; and
- free darning.

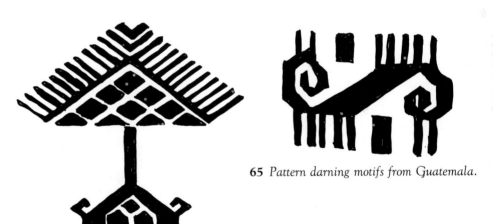

65 *Pattern darning motifs from Guatemala.*

66 *'Part of the Fabric of Society'. Pattern darning on a linen ground to create an image from the book 1984 by George Orwell. (June Linsley)*

58

THREE
Open weaves and structures

Many fabrics have a defined structure, either woven or lock-knit (where the fibres are fixed and cannot be pulled apart). Embroideries which work well on these fabrics exploit the structure and use its geometric qualities to enhance the design.

Fabrics under this heading include:

- canvas;
- hessian;
- hopsack;
- linen of many weights and qualities;
- squared and lacis nets;
- scrim;
- net vegetable bags, etc.;
- loosely woven wool.

There are several techniques which depend on defined warp and weft threads for their success, including hardanger, Assisi and canvas work, but this chapter deals with some very simple techniques which have vast potential:

- darning;
- lacis darning;
- pulled and drawn work;
- needleweaving.

There is also a great deal of potential in distorting and changing the structure of the weaves, and this chapter indicates how this can be tackled.

64 *Darning motifs from Guatemala.*

Stitches

The two main stitches used are cloth stitch (figs 79, 80) and *point de reprise* (78). To begin stitching, make a reef knot at one corner of the mesh. The end may be trimmed off later. Two pieces of thread may also be joined with a reef knot and the ends trimmed later. This technique should look tidy on both sides of the work.

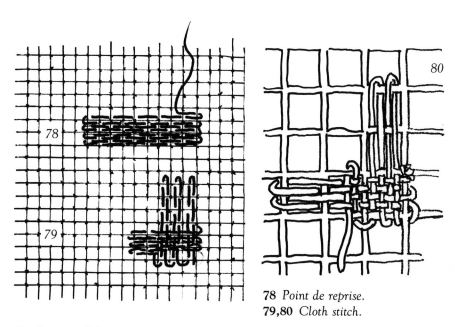

78 *Point de reprise.*
79,80 *Cloth stitch.*

Further possibilities

New effects can be achieved by the addition of dyes or fabrics to the surface.

On some large nets, ribbons and fabrics may be used to darn into the background.

There are some very large scale plastic garden nets which offer exciting possibilities.

81 *Lacis curtain.* Using point de reprise *stitch in fine shaded silk threads, the* fuchsia *pattern has been darned into fine square-mesh curtain net* (Mary Tasker)

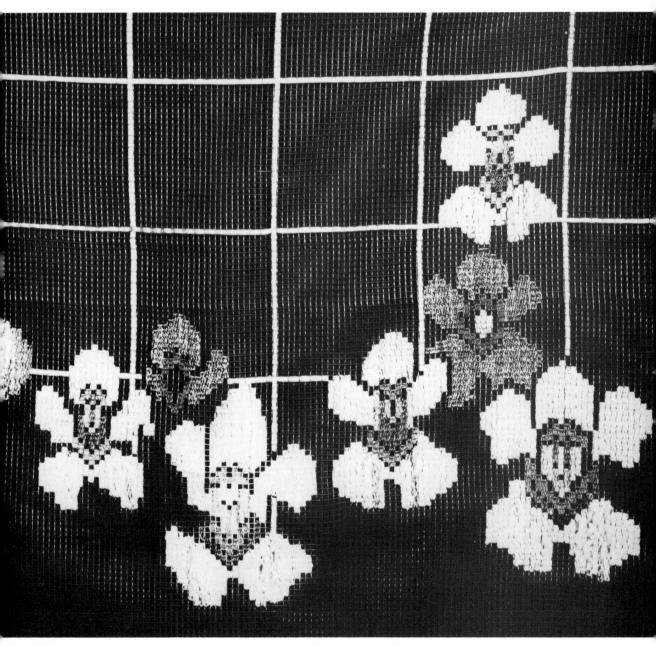

82 *Corner of a tablecloth. Dyed nylon netting has been darned with lustre shaded threads in floral shapes on a grid-like background, in cloth and* point de reprise *stitches. (June Linsley)*

Distorting the weave

A woven fabric can be distorted in a number of ways:

- by prising the threads apart;
- by withdrawing warp or weft threads or a combination of both;
- by pulling into holes or ridges;
- the addition of stitches, threads or fabrics to enhance or exaggerate the pattern of the fabric, including pulled work and needleweaving.

Of the fabrics which can be used successfully in this way, linen scrim of various weights works particularly well.

Pulled work

Conventional pulled work depends on a variety of patterns, achieved by organized groups of stitches which secure the threads in interesting patterns. The simplest of these include satin stitch (fig. 83), eyelets (fig. 84), whipping and overcasting.

These may be freely worked in less formal ways to create dynamic areas of texture.

83 *Satin stitch.*

84 *Eyelet.*

1 'Felt Tiles'. To create this design, based on piles of old tiles, hand-made felt has been dyed, bonded and stitched with hessian, scrim and other fabrics. (*Shirley Crawford*)

2 *Left*: small bag made from hand-woven fabric using a variety of yarns and embroidered with surface stitches. (*Phil Palmer*)
Right: 'Triangular Mosaics'. Bag made from hand-dyed appliquéd silks and gold fabrics with a machine-embroidered hand-made handle. (*Hilary Bower*)

3 'Flower Curtain'. Pieces of free machining worked on hot and cold water dissolve fabrics have been assembled, together with organdie and net inserts, on a hot water dissolve background and machined together. The background was then dissolved away to leave a fragile lace-like fabric. (*June Lovesy*)

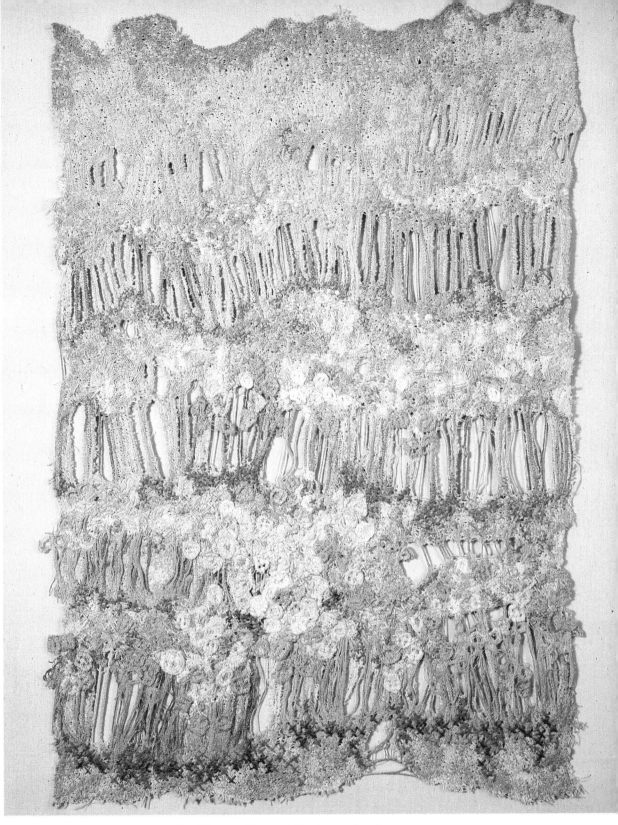

4 'Island Texture – Summer'. Small areas of machine texture worked on scrim in free machine embroidery have been pieced together to form a new fabric. Further machine stitching and hand stitching have been used to blend the pieces and enhance the design. (*Jan Beaney*)

5 Shadow quilting sample. Beads, lace, sequins and threads have been sandwiched between two layers of organdie and backstitched in place. (*Louise Barnes*)

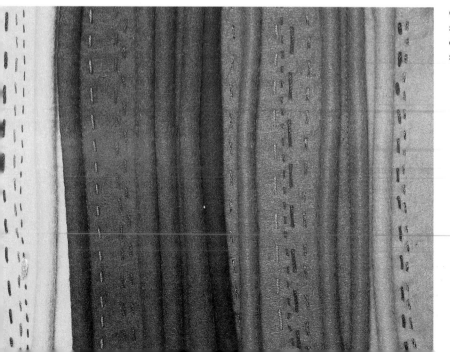

6 Felt sample. To create this colourful sample felt pieces have been joined and decorated with padded ridges and surface stitches. (*Rosemary Jarvis*)

7 'Rouen Cathedral'. A beautiful cathedral in a town with lovely old crumbling buildings forms the basis of this design. Appliqué combined with bonded nets, lace, muslin and surface stitching has been used to convey the impression of decaying architecture.

8 'Reeded Glass Doorway'. Delicate chiffons, nets and organzas have been applied to a plain ground. The resulting fabric has been ridged with machine stitching and slashed along the ridges to create the impression of plants seen through reeded glass. (*Rosemary Jarvis*)

9 'Red Cabbage'. Hand-dyed silk forms the basis of this beautiful cabbage. Each leaf has been quilted and applied to a central core. The edges have been machine stitched and some burning has been used to seal edges. (*Elena Pike*)

10 Pulled scrim pattern. Linen scrim was sprayed with dyes and when dry pulled into holes which were then machine stitched. The motifs in the holes were machine stitched on hot water dissolve fabrics and applied afterwards. (*Lizzie Ettinger*)

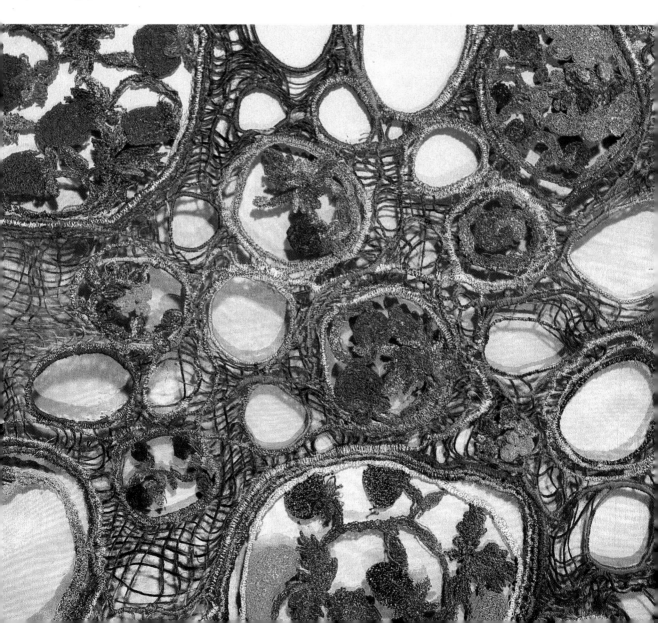

11 Free log cabin piece. The background scrim has been treated with dyes and plaster of Paris. Dyed synthetic fabrics have been applied on the surface with simple couching stitches. (*Cath Parkins*)

12 'Mikado' (detail). The textured fabric blocks comprise nets, organdies and other fabrics bonded together and stitched with free machine embroidery. The fabric was mounted on heavy-duty vilene and applied to a plain ground to form a stylized image based on *The Mikado*. (*Pat Isles*)

85 *Pulled scrim pattern. Linen scrim was sprayed with colours and when dry pulled to create various-sized holes which were then machine stitched in layers. The motifs in the holes were machine stitched on spun alginate and applied afterwards.* (Lizzie Ettinger)

86 *Section of a panel. Threads have been withdrawn from an openweave wool and twisted and fashioned to form patterns. All the dangling threads have been carefully teased from the fabric before being manipulated. (Elaine Bonner)*

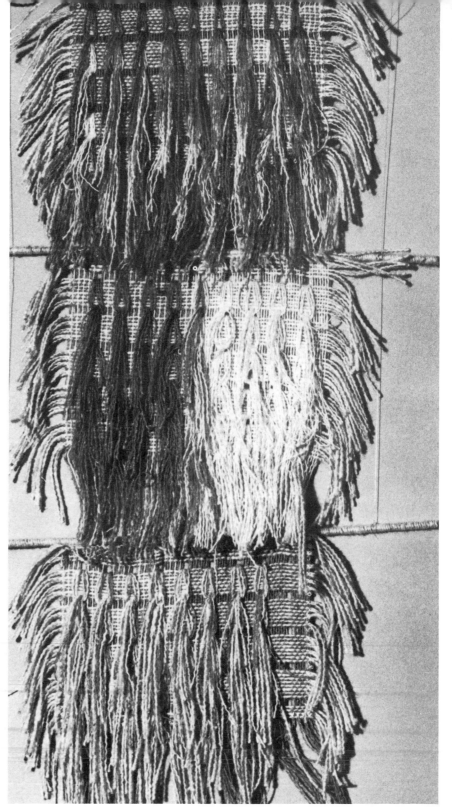

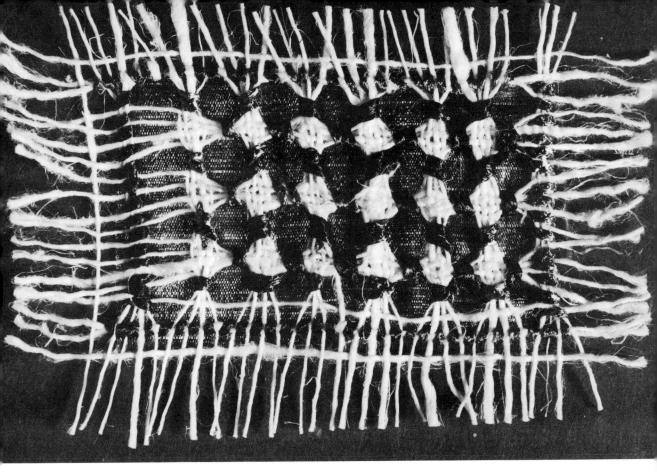

87 *Pulled work sample. Openweave scrim pulled into holes with four-sided stitch, applied to a striped lustre background. (Karen McCarthy)*

88 *Pulled sample. Linen furnishing fabric overcast to pull the fibres into decorative holes. (Sheila Gray)*

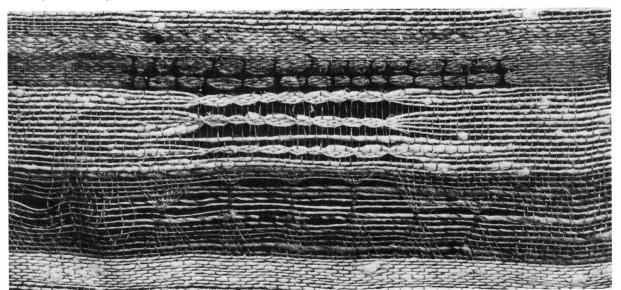

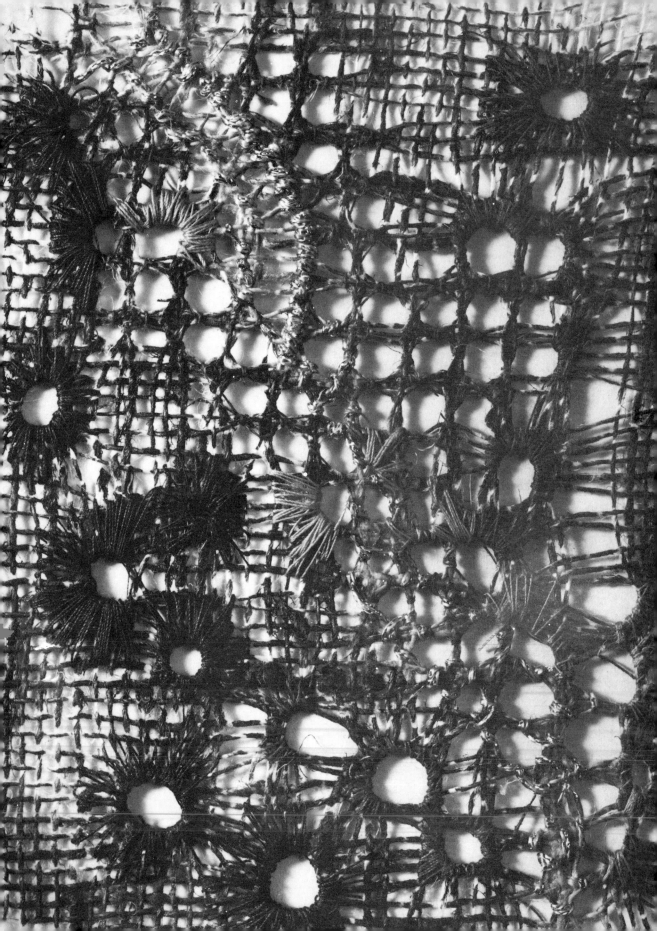

89 *Pulled sample. Open linen scrim sponged with dyes and worked with free eyelets and overcasting in fine threads.* (Sheila Gray)

90 *Pulled sample. A curtain net was used as a ground for this free pulled work. Other weights of fabric have been stitched and applied to the background to form a heavily textured surface.* (Georgina Rees)

91 *Needleweaving. Using checked wool as a foundation fabric, threads were withdrawn and needleweaving worked on the remaining threads to create the legs of the people. Surface stitching has been used to complete the pattern. (June Linsley)*

Needleweaving

Traditional approach

Withdraw the necessary warp or weft threads and secure them. For household articles which need to wash and wear, the ends must be secured by darning in or by buttonhole stitching. Any extra ends should be trimmed off. The threads over which the needleweaving will be worked may be hemstitched (fig. 92) to add strength and organize them into groups. For purely decorative work this is not necessary.

Carry out the needleweaving in a figure of eight over and under the groups of threads, using a thread of similar weight and quality to the background (fig. 93).

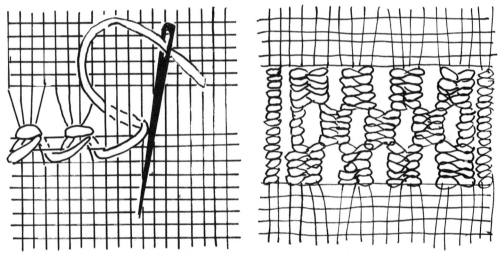

92 *Hemstitching.*　　　93 *Needleweaving.*

Free needleweaving

It is possible to work on threads which have been prised apart or withdrawn in less controlled patterns. Threads can be laid on the surface of the fabric and needleweaving worked into them. In this way several layers may be built up to good effect for designs based on natural forms (see page 80).

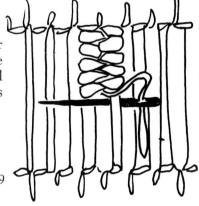

94 *Needleweaving in progress.*

79

95 *Needleweaving. On an openweave ground, needleweaving has been freely worked and further threads laid over the top to create different layers of needleweaving. (Jane Clarke)*

Canvas

Canvas is a fabric with a strongly defined rigid mesh. It has been customary to cover the surface completely with stitches. Instead of treating it as fabric to be explored, people tend to have preconceived ideas of what canvas work should look like and allow themselves to be too influenced by what they have seen before.

Ways of exploring canvas include:

- using a variety of threads such as torn fabrics and ribbons;
- leaving parts of the fabric unworked;
- incorporating it with other techniques;
- mixing different types and mesh size of canvas in one piece of work;
- the use of dyes and areas of appliqué and stitches not normally associated with canvas work, such as raised chain band.

96 *'Canvas Landscape'. On a canvas ground, tent stitch and tufting have been freely worked in a variety of threads and torn fabrics. Parts of the canvas have deliberately been left unworked. (Linda Chilton)*

81

97 *'No Traycloths at Greenham Common'. June Linsley says of this piece of work; 'I was very moved by the writer's regret that she had never thanked her suffragette mother for her sacrifices, but taken for granted the freedom the suffragettes had secured for all women. She went on to point out that suffragettes were reviled, mocked, and maltreated, yet without them all women would still be tyrannized by Mrs Thatcher's beloved Victorian values, and Mrs Thatcher would not be in 10 Downing Street, decrying the peace women.*

I began with a formal white work grid pattern symbolizing the repression of convention, then showed how the suffragettes distorted this grid and broke through it as free women. Peace campaigners besiege from the outside of the grid which guards the most deadly weapons of our time. The white work became suffused with the green and purple of the suffragette colours, then the full spectrum was introduced, rainbow colours which symbolize peace, and after which the different peace camps are named.'

This piece was worked on rug canvas. (June Linsley)

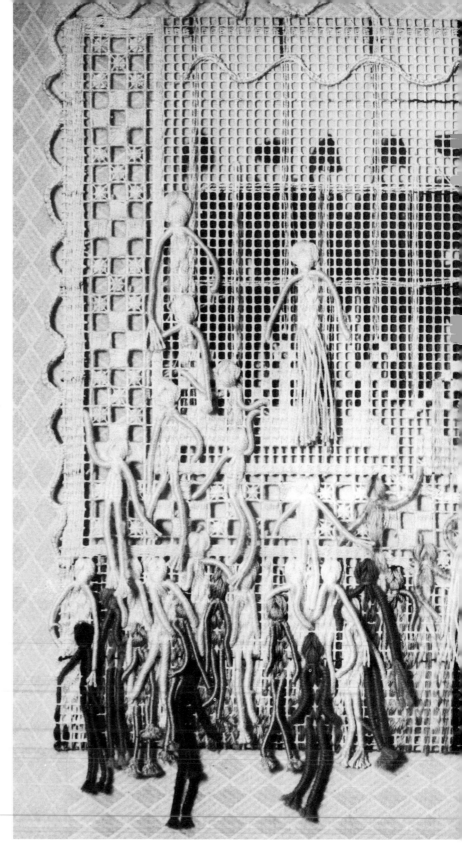

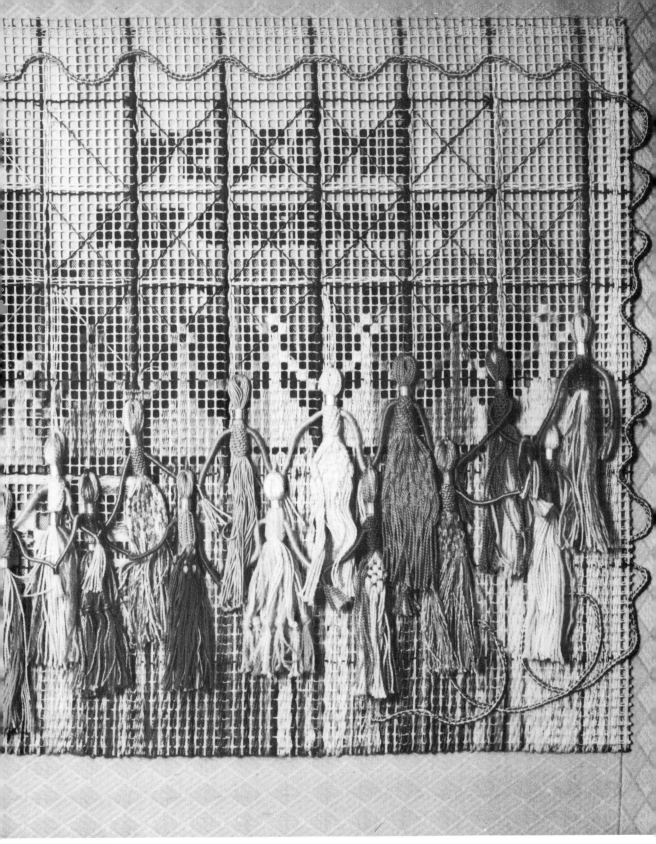

FOUR

Patterned and textured fabrics

In recent years there has been a tendency to reject patterned fabrics in favour of plain unadorned materials. Non-patterned fabrics offer a 'blank canvas' on which to stitch and dye. A limited number of embroiderers have continued to work successfully with patterned fabrics, but they have been most widely used in patchwork.

Fabrics with strong characteristics, either of pattern or of pile, have a visual effect which demands attention. This may well detract from other aspects of a design and dominate, so great care must be taken in their use.

Strongly patterned fabrics can provide the starting point for exciting ideas, and this section deals with some of the possibilities of fabrics easily available in local shops. These include:

- stripes;
- checks and ginghams;
- spots;
- velvets and fabrics with pile;
- corded and ridged fabrics;
- shot fabrics.

As with other experimental work, a notebook recording ideas for the future, with scraps of fabric and worked samples, will prove invaluable. Quick samples may be backed with iron-on interfacing and stuck rather than sewn, to gain an impression of the effect.

98 *Fabric sample based on a theme of decay. A variety of fabrics, including broderie anglaise, have been combined with surface stitching which reflects the patterns in the broderie anglaise. (Ann Marchbanks)*

Stripes

There are many types of striped fabric available. They range from sheer synthetics with delicate lustred threads, to school uniform stripes and, at the extreme end, deckchair stripes. The stripes may be even, or may vary in width and spacing.

Design
Striped wrapping paper or hand-drawn striped paper are useful for designing. Cut up the paper into shapes and place them one on top of another, turning at different angles to get the effect of contrasts. Circles and squares make the most effective patterns. From these simple beginnings more complex designs based on landscapes and natural forms may suggest themselves. The designs may then be carried out in a number of techniques including patchwork and appliqué.

Spots and checks

As with stripes, spots and checks have a strong dramatic effect which can take over a design unless used sensitively and deliberately. They can be employed to great effect in simple patterns which exploit their visual impact.

99 *Bag. Large bugle beads criss-cross on a striped fabric to create a dynamic pattern.* (Mary Shea)

100 *Sample from a notebook. Striped fabrics interwoven with hessian, felt and surface stitches. (Rosemary Jarvis)*

101 *Cushions. Striped ticking and black cotton in various combinations to create patterns based on zebra stripes, using machine appliqué. (Joan Knowles)*

102 *Samples exploring the possibilities of striped fabric.*

103 *Combinations of techniques based on spotted fabric.*

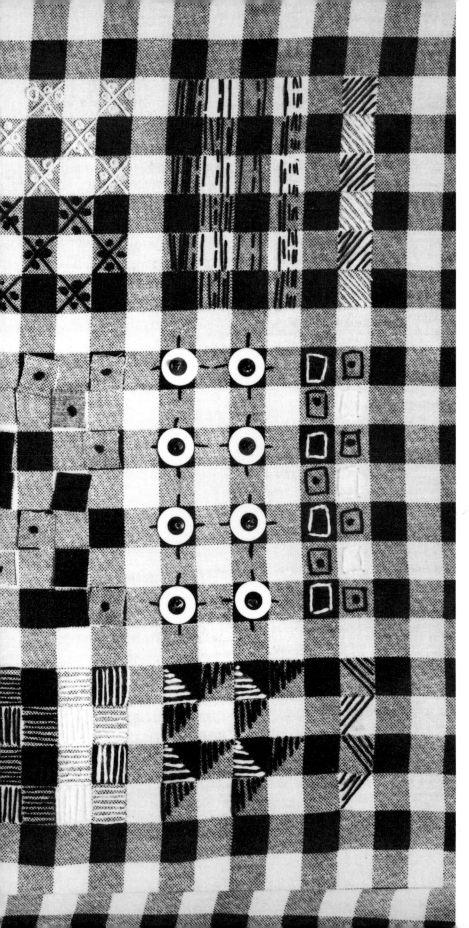

104 *Fabric sample based on a cotton gingham.*

Corded and ridged fabrics

Corded and ridged fabrics also have strong though more subtle visual effects.

Corded fabrics can be made from silk or synthetic fibres. They have the double feature of a strong ridge and a pile which reflects different tones depending on the direction of the light. When planning clothes or domestic articles, it is essential to make sure that the pile lies in the same direction if joining two or more pieces together. This disadvantage may be used positively in embroidery, where subtle tone changes may benefit the design. The ridges can be used for stitching and for sandwiching beads, etc. Other fabrics such as furnishing reps and some knitted fabrics also feature stripes, and it is possible to create ridges in fabrics by means of tucks or with the twin needle on a sewing machine.

105 *Seascape sampler. Bugle beads, stitching and frayed fibres on a dyed needlecord ground.*

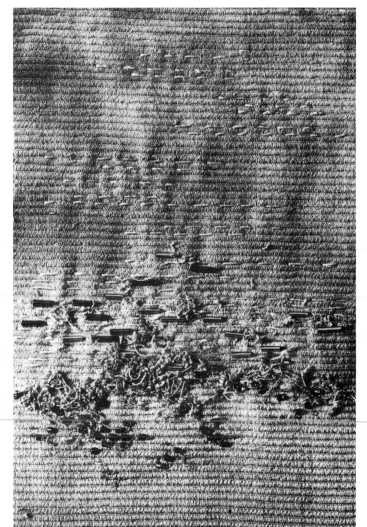

FACING PAGE
106 *Corduroy sampler. Exercises illustrating the tonal effects which may be achieved by turning the fabric to exaggerate the play of light on the surface.*

107 *'Nineteen-thirties Lady'.*
Stitching and applied fabrics
have been worked on a
patterned ground to create the
impression of a knitted
cardigan, lace collar and
dress. The dress fabric
pattern has been enhanced by
tiny eyelets. (Ann Sutton)

Patterned fabrics

There are thousands of patterned fabrics in the soft furnishings and dressmaking departments of local stores. Where a patterned fabric is needed it is of course possible to print your own in a variety of ways.

When using such fabric in an embroidery, always stand well back and make sure that it enhances rather than detracts from the design. The two examples featured in figs 107 and 108 demonstrate the sensitive use of appropriate patterned fabric in designs.

108 'Unmade Bed'. Ticking was used as a ground fabric, combined with cotton and blanket edging – including the label. The cathedral window patchwork features a fine cotton patterned fabric in scale with the design. (Lynda Watts)

109 *Velvet sample. The edges of the velvet pieces have been singed, twisted and applied with the addition of blanket stitch. (Shirley Warren)*

Velvets

Velvets of all types have a compelling appearance and demand attention. Stitching into velvet can result in a messy finish, as the stitches may become lost. Of the techniques which work, appliqué and quilting are the simplest.

Transfer of design is best worked by tacking through tissue paper on to the velvet and then tearing the tissue paper carefully away. Other velvets such as panne velvet and crushed velvet have a flatter pile and a lustrous surface which may be used with dyes and softer stitches. Because they are not as raised as ordinary velvet they are more easily manipulated.

Dyeing velvet needs careful thought in order to penetrate the pile without flattening it. Spraying works well but the dye tends to sit on the surface.

110 *Section of a quilted jacket. On to a synthetic velvet, dyes have been sprayed and machine quilting worked in lustre threads. (Gail Harker)*

111 *Reflections. To represent the reflections in mirror-glass office windows, rectangular shapes were quilted and joined together with buttonhole bars. Synthetic shot organzas in layers have enhanced the images and reflect the light in interesting ways.* (Judith Smalley)

Shot fabrics

FACING PAGE
112 *Shot silk sample page. Shot silk turned and applied in different directions to reflect the play of light. The different tones on this sample have been achieved with one fabric only.*

Shot fabrics are those which have warp and weft of a different colour. This results in a surface which changes in tone according to the play of light. The effects are subtle and delicate and work particularly well in patchwork. For household articles it is usually advisable to keep the grain of the fabric in the same direction, but with shot fabrics the disadvantages of doing so are outweighed by the contrasting tonal differences revealed by the play of light.

FIVE

Making fabrics

With so many fabrics available for embroidery, it might seem unnecessary to consider methods of constructing them.

There are times, however, when it is not possible to obtain just the right fabric for a particular design. Rather than compromise, you may find a home-made fabric will prove more satisfactory. It is also very rewarding to have total control over a piece of embroidery from the making of the ground fabric through to the completed piece.

A dissatisfaction with readymade fabrics has been a feature of much professional and student work during the 1970s and 1980s. Students have been encouraged to look at the structure of fabrics in order to ensure that the work they do on and with them is really appropriate and not just superficial decoration.

Many embroiderers might have considered making their own fabrics but thought the techniques required studio equipment out of their reach. In fact some of the fabrics can be easily made in the home, the main requirement being a willingness to experiment and benefit from some failures along the way.

As with other experimental work, a notebook recording all your experiments will be of tremendous benefit. Even the disappointments can be looked on positively, as they point out pitfalls to avoid in the future. In this chapter some of the basic methods are set out to whet the appetite and indicate some further possibilities.

Should any technique particularly appeal to you, you can gain expertise and confidence from continual experiments. The bibliography at the end of the book contains the names of specialist books and pamphlets. Some of these books also name groups who share your interests and with whom you can exchange ideas. The techniques considered in this chapter include:

- knitting;
- weaving;
- felting; and
- machine-made lace-like fabrics.

113 *Section of a jacket. Flattened, knotted and dyed rouleaus of fabric were joined together with freely worked insertion stitches to create a new fabric for a fitted jacket.* (Margaret Potts)

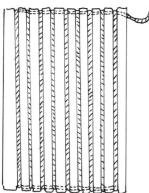

114 *Simple card loom.*

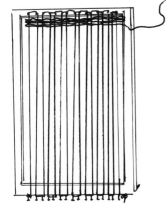

115 *Wooden frame loom.*

Woven backgrounds

Weaving has a long history as a method of producing a fabric for both domestic and decorative use. It is often a lengthy and highly skilled process involving specialist equipment, but some worthwhile results can be achieved with simple weaving frames. Improvised frames using thick card (fig. 114) or a wooden rectangular frame (fig. 115) work well.

Run the warp threads from top to bottom of the frame as in figs 114, 115. These threads form the basis of the fabric and should be strong enough to remain taut during the process.

Using a weaving needle or shuttle, work the weft threads to and fro alternately over and under the warp threads until complete. As this is experimental, it may not be necessary to ensure the threads are firmly packed together, and you may like to make the gaps a feature of the design.

To vary the effects a variety of threads can be combined:

- shiny/matt;
- thick/thin;
- knobbly/smooth;
- torn fabrics, etc.

The resulting textile may hang or be applied to the surface of another fabric to enrich the texture. If it is to hang independently, the ends must be secured by darning into the weaving or tying off carefully and perhaps fringing.

By using pre-dyed strips, interesting colour combinations may be achieved.

116 *Woven sample. Wires covered with dyed sheeps' wool, net and bound threads have been interwoven to form a fabric.* (Gail Harker)

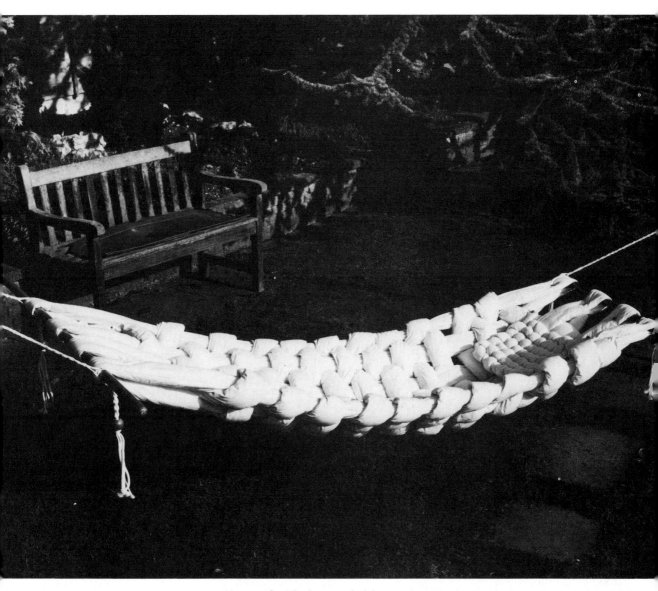

117 *Hammock. The hammock fabric is formed of a continuous tube of calico with a wadding filling. The resulting large-scale yarn was woven to create a flexible comfortable fabric to lie on. The pillow has been constructed in a similar way, on a smaller scale. (Jane Clarke)*

118 *'. . . and love is proved in the letting go'. A poem by C. Day Lewis was the inspiration for this hanging. The 'letting go' begins at birth. Hessian, scrim, etc., were bleached and dyed, then interwoven and applied to a background to form the basis of the panel. (Sue Brown)*

106

Felt making

Felt making is an ancient technique with a history of at least 3000 years. The felt sold for embroidery has the reputation of a luridly coloured, unsophisticated fabric, although, as pointed out in an earlier section, this is undeserved.

Hand-made felt has a quality which can be bold or delicate and varied in texture according to the way it is made. It is a light, warm material which resists water.

Wool is one of the few fibres which possesses the property of being able to felt. The process involves the controlled application of hot and cold water combined with friction and pressure. The fibres react to being deliberately shocked by combining with each other to form a fabric. Many of us will have inadvertently felted wool in a washing machine, resulting in a rigid piece of material!

Method
Using natural unwashed fibres from a sheep's fleece, work the following method:

1 Card or tease the fibres so that they lie in the same direction, and place a layer on a flat dry surface (figs 119, 120).
2 Lay a second layer (batt) of teased or carded fibres on the first layer at right angles (fig. 121). If a firm, regular edge is required, make sure the thickness of the felt is maintained right to the edge.
3 Build up the layers, each one at right angles to the previous layer. As a rough guide, four layers of batting about 5 cm thick produce felt of approximately 2 cm.
4 Enclose the completed flat batt in a fabric envelope. For large pieces a pillowcase is suitable, but muslin and sheeting also work well. Secure the layers together with large stitches to prevent the felt from slipping during the process (fig. 122). A polythene bag with holes in to allow water to run in and out may also be used.

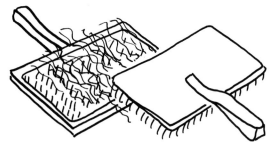

119 *Using carders to tease the wool.*

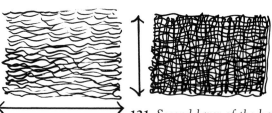

120 *First layer of the batt.*

121 *Second layer of the batt.*

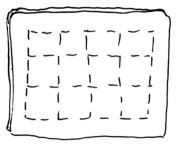

122 *Batt enclosed in muslin.*

123 *Batt on a reed mat.*

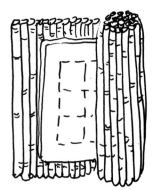

124 *Batt rolled in a reed mat.*

5 Place the flat batt in a bowl or other container.
6 Add washing-up liquid to boiling water (two or three squeezes will suffice) and pour over the batt.
7 Remove from the bowl and pound with a rolling pin or similar object. Roll it over a rough surface, if possible.
8 Using a ridged flexible rush mat, place the batt on the mat and roll them both up (fig. 124). Then squeeze them together and wring as firmly as possible. Remove the batt from the mat, place in the bowl and apply cold water. Repeat the pounding, rolling, squeezing and wringing.
9 Continue alternately applying hot and cold water until the desired finish is required.
10 Leave to dry naturally.

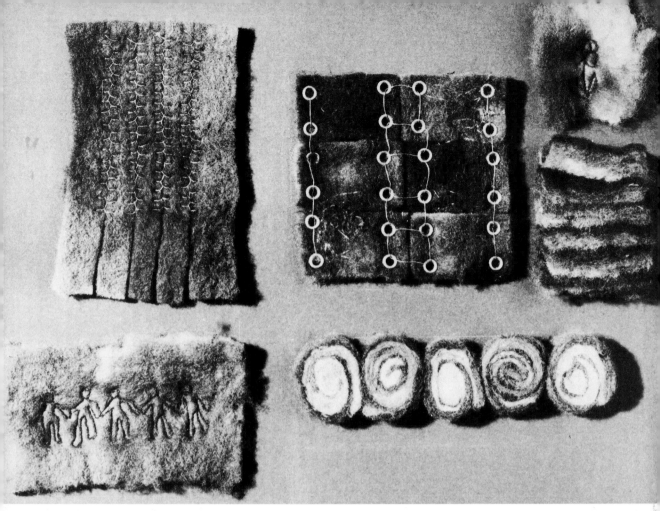

125 *Felt samples. Hand-made felt samples demonstrating how felt may be dyed, joined, sandwiched and stitched. (June Linsley)*

The more of this shock treatment the felt receives the firmer it will become. Large pieces may be worked in the bath, although boiling water is more effective than hot tap water. Stamping on it may help to felt the fibres. It is a very physical process and although it is also time-consuming, lovely surfaces may be achieved.

Keep notes on the process. Different fleeces will have different matting properties, even in the same species of sheep. Record for future reference the number of layers you have used and how many water applications you have made.

FACING PAGE
126 *Felt jacket section. On a dyed, hand-made felt ground, intricate patterns have been worked with machine stitching, throwing up the unworked areas as in quilting. (June Linsley)*

Dyes can be added with the water during the felting process. Other fibres such as ribbons, yarns and pieces of fabric may be added between the layers, but it must be remembered that they will not have the same felting properties. They will be held in place by the wool fibres. When the felt is complete, other decoration may suggest itself.

Fine felt may be easier to stitch into if first tacked to another fabric, and muslin works well for this as it is soft and flexible.

110

127 *'Memories Landscape'. A dyed and stitched landscape has been enclosed in a hand-made felt frame, held in position by further decorative surface stitching. (Sue Brown)*

128 *'Sheep'. On a hand-made felt ground, the sheep have been worked in stump work techniques and frayed fabrics applied for the pasture. (Barbara Hirst)*

Knitting

Recent years have seen the growth of knitting as a truly creative means of making surfaces. It is not always an advantage to be a skilled knitter, as years spent perfecting an even technique may inhibit a free and less controlled approach. Knitting can be expanded in a variety of ways.

Possibilities for experimental knitting:

- mixing of a wide variety of yarns in one piece;
- changing needle size within the same piece;
- deliberate dropping of stitches to disrupt the evenness of the surface;
- in a technique pioneered by Jan Messent, knitting out in different directions from a starting point has many possibilities. It grows rather like a natural form;
- the addition of beads and stitches to the surface;
- the blending of knitted pieces with other techniques.

Fashion garments have recently featured ribbon knitting or knitting with tapes or torn strips of fabric.

In order to make balls of fabric.strips, take a piece of fabric and trim off the corners. Cut the fabric in a spiral continuous strip which avoids too many joins in the knitting.

Some garishly patterned fabrics have a more subtle look when cut up and treated in this way. It is even possible to knit plastic. Fraying fabrics have a delightful surface when knitted.

Knitting has a strong texture and can dominate a piece, so care should be taken to use it sensitively with other forms of embroidery.

129 *Knitted sample. A freely knitted sample using a variety of yarns into which surface stitching has been added, making a very rich texture.* (Henrietta Curtis)

130 *Knitted jacket. The jacket fabric has been constructed from areas of knitted texture, using a variety of yarns. Further surface stitching has been added as the fabric was pieced together. (Elaine Bonner)*

131 *'Delphinium Panel'. The panel has been made in three layers. The central part features transfer dyes and machine embroidery. The next layer is a quilted frame with painted delphinium flowers. The outer frame has been knitted in chunky knitting yarns and strips of fabric. Additional hand stitching and detached leaves were added afterwards. (Julia Barton)*

Fabrics made with the sewing machine

Developments with dissolve techniques on the sewing machine are happening so fast that any advice is subject to new products on the market.

In principle, this technique involves stitching on to a background and then dissolving the background away, leaving the structure of the stitches to form a new fabric. This is most frequently used for lace-like motifs which can be applied to other work, but it is possible to construct large areas in this way. The main technical point to be considered when working a dissolve technique is to stitch the motif or fabric with an underlying structure of machine running stitch, as zig-zag alone does not hold together when the background has been dissolved away.

Set the machine controls for free running stitch and either frame the fabric or use a darning foot.

Method 1: vanishing muslin
Work stitching on to the vanishing muslin ground, and when complete iron the fabric on a hot setting. The background disintegrates, leaving the stitching. It will also crumble if placed in an oven. Sometimes fibres of the vanishing muslin are difficult to destroy, and they can be an effective addition to the appearance.

Method 2: acetate dissolve
Use acetate fabric as a background. Not all shop assistants are aware of the composition of their fabrics, so be sure to test a sample first. Work the stitching on the acetate fabric; trim away the excess background.

Place work in a bowl of acetone (the fumes can be very strong, so make sure your room is well ventilated). The acetate will gradually dissolve away, leaving the stitching. With large or heavily encrusted areas of stitching more than one dip may be necessary.

The solution may become saturated and a fresh bowlful be required.

Whilst wet, the stitching may be manipulated into a shape which it will maintain when dry.

Method 3: spun alginate dissolve (hot water dissolve)
This fabric can be used in a similar way to acetate. When the stitching has been completed, trim off the excess and place the work in an ovenproof glass bowl. Then pour boiling water over it.

It shrivels in an alarming way, but when the spun alginate has dissolved (this may take more than one application of hot water), and the stitching has been pinned out to dry, it will return to shape.

Method 4: cold water dissolve
Stitching should be worked on the background fabric (see list of suppliers). Trim off the excess fabric. Pour cold water over the work and dissolve the background away.

Please note that with methods 3 and 4 the pieces which have been trimmed off may be joined together to form a piece of fabric which can in turn be stitched on, thus avoiding wastage.

132 *'Daisy Bag'. Machine stitching on spun alginate (hot water dissolve fabric) forms the fabric of the bag. The machine texture has been mounted on a silver lamé contrasting ground which twinkles through. (Jan Beaney)*

133 *'Flower Curtain'. Pieces of free machining worked on hot and cold water dissolve fabrics were assembled, together with organdie and net inserts, on to a hot water dissolve background and machined together. The background was then dissolved away to leave a fragile lace-like fabric. (June Lovesy)*

Patching and piecing

The joining together of two or more pieces of fabric is an obvious method of creating a new fabric, and has a long history. Early weaving techniques produced narrow bands of fabric which had to be joined together to make clothes, etc.

Traditional patchwork is a well documented technique, but there are some aspects of patching and piecing fabrics together in a less formal manner which create exciting surfaces.

Formal patchwork relies on the accurate cutting and joining of pieces of sympathetic fabric, but less regular pieces in contrasting materials may be used where the resulting decorative piece does not have to be washed. Seam lines can be blended with stitches or used to further the design.

There are many occasions when it is difficult to find a single piece of fabric which is entirely suitable for a design. A simple landscape could be built up in even or uneven strips reflecting the shapes, and this used as a basis for appliqué or further stitching. Shiny and matt surfaces can be combined in this way to create a unique background. The examples of patching and piecing on pages 122 and 123 demonstrate the effective use of this technique to create wholly original fabrics.

SIX

Experimental materials for embroidery

I use the word 'materials' here to indicate the range of sometimes unlikely fabrics or objects which are being used for embroidery in the present experimental climate. This subject causes controversy, and it is an argument which has no true conclusion, since so much depends on personal opinion.

'But is it embroidery?' is a question which is frequently asked as the boundaries of embroidery are expanded. At contemporary exhibitions artists have made use of wood, plaster, paper, wire, foam and plastic to help interpret their designs, and many people find this unacceptable. Yet we know from our knowledge of historical embroideries that all manner of strange materials have been included in the past. Perhaps a more appropriate question would be: 'Does it work in the context in which it has been used?'

Many pieces of work which include 'found objects' such as wood, shells or feathers are unsuccessful because they do nothing to further the harmony of the design. To include unusual materials simply to be different is obviously not sufficient on its own.

There are occasions, however, when the designer has spotted the potential of a seemingly unlikely material and worked it in harmoniously. There is a strong tendency to experiment and break down the barriers between the various art forms, and to go against accepted traditions. This is bound to cause controversy, but it injects fresh blood into the subject and encourages us to reassess our views from time to time. Not all of it succeeds, but some delightful pieces of embroidery have resulted from this willingness to experiment. An exhibition which merely reinforces one's assumptions and does not pose any new questions is often dull. It is good to sharpen the critical faculties and consider new developments with an open mind.

The next few pages contain some examples of work which have incorporated unusual or unexpected materials.

FACING PAGE
136 *Dried bullrushes, stitched together with a variety of yarns in free herringbone stitch.* (Geraldine Ormonde)

WHITE COLLAR WORKERS

Shell patchwork, folded fabric and padded felt shapes

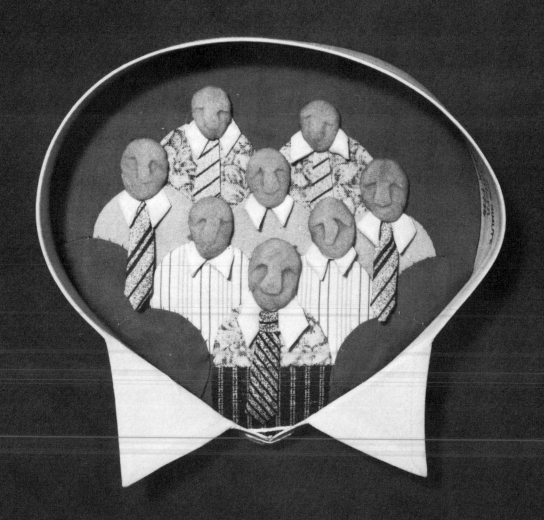

137 *'White Collar Workers'. An old white stiff collar formed the basis of this sample, combined with quilted and paper figures. (June Linsley)*

138 *'Lark Rise to Candleford'. To create an image from the book of this title, scrim, sealing wax, paper, old newspaper, stamps and dried flowers have been combined with surface stitching. (Ann Cunningham)*

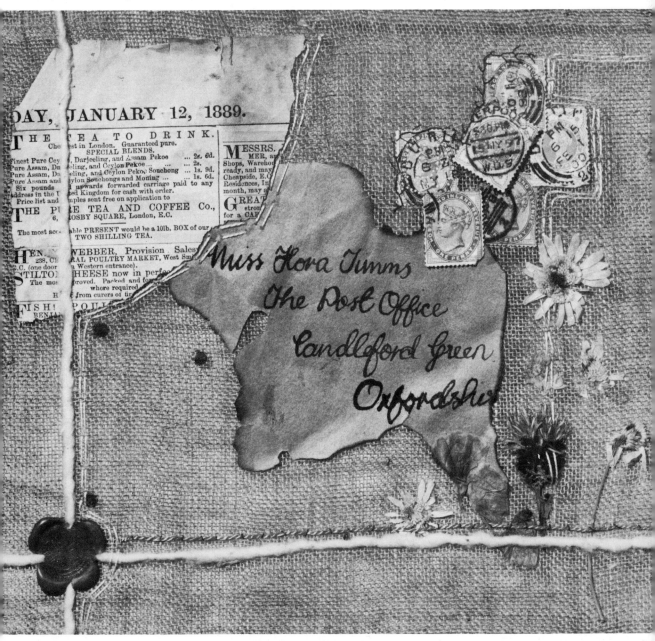

139 *'Beach Scene'. A piece of hand-made paper formed the idea for this piece of work. The figures, made from tights, have been applied to the ground using dressmakers' bonding adhesive. The beach has been applied to tarlatan and stitched to wooden struts to form a windbreak. The deckchair features a seascape darned into hessian. (Phil Palmer)*

140 *Page from a 'Fabric Notebook'. Couched threads on a fabric combining muslin and plaster of Paris. (Cath Parkins)*

141 *Decorative fan. Machine embroidery on soluble fabrics has been applied to a wrapped wire base and combined with moulded silk birds and shells made from paper pulp and silk threads. (Linda Chilton)*

142 *'Normandy Fragment'. This sample, based on old Normandy walls and a street flower stall, has been worked on a piece of worn fabric picked up on a beach after a long period in the sea.*

Fabrics and their properties

Name of fabric	Composition	Properties
acetate	man-made	dissolves in acetone so can be used for fabric dissolve technique
acrylic	man-made, often blended with other fibres and used to make wool-like fabrics	bulky, hard to touch, adds hard-wearing qualities to natural fibres
brocade	satin or mixture	raised designs on a contrasting surface, often with gold or silver threads
burlap	usually jute but also hemp or flax	coarse, loosely woven
calico	cotton	off-white, various weights, manipulates well, many uses
cambric	flax or cotton	fine, evenweave
cashmere	wool from mountain goat or wild Himalayan sheep	fine, soft, easy-to-manipulate fabric
canvas	hemp, cotton and others	lattice-like square mesh of various sizes, used for canvas work and other embroidery techniques
cheesecloth	cotton	thin, not too closely woven
chiffon	silk or synthetic	soft, delicate, sheer
corduroy	usually cotton or cotton and polyester	ribbed woven fabric, raised cut pile with high and low surfaces
cotton	cotton (plant)	absorbent, good for dyes and manipulation, soft when washed
crash	cotton, linen	fine or coarse, rough irregular surface, various weights; useful all-purpose fabric
crêpe	wool, silk, synthetic or a combination	crinkled surface, slightly elastic
crêpe de Chine	silk or rayon	fine, delicate
damask	silk, cotton, rayon or man-made	reversible, woven with patterns, often self-coloured
denim	cotton	twill-weave, very strong and stiff

Name of fabric	Composition	Properties
felt	wool	non-woven pressed fabric, non-fraying; manipulates well
flannel	cotton or wool	soft with a fuzzy nap
gabardine	cotton, blends of wool, polyester or rayon	fine diagonal ribs, firm, wears well
gauze	cotton	sheer, fine
gingham	cotton	closely woven, evenweave in checks, plaids or stripes
hopsack	cotton, linen or rayon	loosely woven, medium-weight
hessian	hemp or jute	coarse strong cloth useful for stitching
huckaback	linen	woven fabric with a loose thread which can be used for huckaback darning
jersey	silk, wool, cotton, nylon, rayon, etc.	smooth knitted fabrics of various weights, manipulates well
lamé	metallic threads sometimes combined with others, often synthetic	for specialized uses, where a shiny surface is required
lawn	cotton	sheer, fine, delicate
leather	skin of animals, birds or reptiles	hard-wearing, fine or coarse, thick or thin, shiny front, rough back; usually tough to sew
linen	flax	evenweave, variety of weights; suitable for counted thread techniques, creases easily
muslin	cotton	fine, soft openweave, used as a backing for quilting; dyes and manipulates beautifully
needlecord	cotton, silk or synthetic	finely ribbed corduroy
net	cotton, silk, nylon	delicate, fine mesh
nylon	synthetic	very strong, variety of weights including sheer; resilient, resists creases

Name of fabric	Composition	Properties
organdie	cotton	sheer, fine, stiff; suitable for shadow work, etc.
organza	silk, synthetic	fine, sheer, delicate; softer than organdie
panne velvet	cotton, silk, synthetic	velvet pressed to give a smooth sheen; soft and pliable
plush	usually man-made	coarse, velvet-type fabric with channels between the weave
polyester	man-made	crease-resistant, washable, retains its shape, accepts transfer dyes well
poplin	cotton, cotton and polyester mix	closely woven, strong
satin	silk, cotton, polyester	shiny, slippery, various weights
scrim	linen, cotton or mixture	fine or coarse, openweave, excellent for pulling holes and manipulation; contains dressing so moulds well when damp
seersucker	cotton	crinkly, bubbly surface, lightweight
silk	silkworm thread	warm, strong, resilient, closely woven; a variety of weights, some with a pronounced sheen, others dull, smooth or textured Jap silk – sheer, very delicate; dyes beautifully
taffeta	silk, polyester, nylon	closely woven, crisp, lustrous
ticking	cotton or linen	closely woven, usually striped, very strong; often used as a covering for pillows, bolsters and mattresses
tulle	silk, cotton, synthetic	fine, delicate mesh
tweed	wool	closely woven, bulky
velvet	silk, cotton or synthetic	closely woven, short-cut pile
Vilene*	fused – usually synthetic	stiffening, sometimes with adhesive to be ironed on to fabric
Viyella*	cotton and wool	soft, easy to manipulate, suitable for smocking, etc.

Name of fabric	Composition	Properties
voile	cotton	fine, transparent, soft; drapes and handles well
wool	sheep, goat or rabbit hair, etc.	warm, absorbent, elastic, soft; closely or loosely woven, doesn't crease easily, dyes well
worsted	wool	special long twisted wool, strong, smooth and firm

* brand name

Glossary of terms

backing one fabric placed behind another to add strength, useful in some types of quilting and bead work or metal thread work.

bias/bias cut diagonal line in relation to the warp and weft of the fabric – the direction in which the fabric stretches. (*True bias* – an exact diagonal of 45 degrees to the warp and weft.)

bonding method of joining or fusing two fabrics by means of plastic adhesive inserted between the two, to which heat is applied.

breadth the width of the fabric from selvage to selvage.

brushed with the nap (surface) raised by brushing.

cloth fabric made by any method.

conservation preservation of textiles to preserve them from damage and deterioration.

counted thread term used for a variety of embroidery techniques requiring an evenweave fabric so that the threads may be counted.

cross cut on the cross – see *true bias*.

dressing size, glaze or other stiffening used in finishing textiles.

fabric a structure or construction, frequently referring to woven materials.

grafting the invisible joining of two pieces of material, used in techniques such as canvas work or knitting.

grain along the line of the warp threads in woven fabrics.

ground main body of the fabric.

hem a turning on the edge of a piece of fabric, which is sewn to prevent fraying.

knitted textile formed by interlocking a series of loops of yarns or thread in a continuous pattern.

man-made fabrics derived from the regenerated fibres of natural origin such as triacetates or rayons.

material   matter from which a thing is made – often used to describe fabrics of various types.

matt   without lustre.

mesh   a network or interlaced structure with open spaces, such as net.

nap   surface of a cloth which has raised fibres – usually a soft surface.

natural fibres   fibres derived from vegetable or animal fibres such as linen (flax) or cashmere (goat).

pile   a raised soft surface to a fabric, produced by weaving in extra yarns or knotting them into the surface.

pinking   decoration of a raw edge of fabric with serrations. It also prevents fraying.

puckering   areas of fabric which do not lie flat because they have been stitched too tightly or pulled unevenly.

raw edge   an unfinished edge of a cut fabric.

selvage (selvedge)   the edge of a piece of fabric, woven in such a way that the weft will not unravel.

sheer   a fabric which is thin enough to be transparent.

shot fabric   fabric with warp and weft of different colours, so that the colour changes according to the direction of the light.

slub   a lump or thick area in a yarn or thread which produces an irregularity on the surface of the fabric.

stretching   the process of smoothing or squaring a piece of embroidery by placing it face uppermost on a dampened board and pinning into shape so that it may be mounted or framed.

synthetic   an artificially produced fabric such as nylon or Terylene.

textile   a general term used for any fabric produced by weaving a variety of fibres.

texture   this term originally applied to weaving, but is now used to describe the quality of surface: the thickness, smoothness, roughness, etc.

twill   a weave in which the yarns interlace and create a diagonal rib.

union a fabric which has the warp of one basic material and weft of another.

warp threads stretching lengthwise on a loom.

weft threads crossing from side to side of a loom at right angles to, and interweaving with, the warp threads.

width measurement from side to side; a piece of material of the woven width.

woven type of fabric formed by interlacing a continuous thread back and forth across a set of lengthwise threads.

Bibliography

BEANEY, Jan *Embroidery: New Approaches* Pelham
—— *Stitches: New Approaches* Batsford
CAMPBELL-HARDING, Valerie *Strip Patchwork* Batsford
CAVE, Œnone, and HODGES, Jean *Smocking: Traditional and Modern Approaches* Batsford
CLABBURN, Pamela *The Needleworker's Dictionary* Macmillan
EMBROIDERERS' GUILD PRACTICAL STUDY GROUP *Needlework School* Windward
GRAY, Jennifer *Canvas Work* Batsford
HOWARD, Constance *Embroidery and Colour* Batsford
JOHN, Edith *Needleweaving* Batsford
MCNEILL, Moyra *Machine Embroidery: Lace and See-Through Techniques* Batsford
—— *Pulled Thread* Mills & Boon
MELEN, Lisa *Knotting and Netting* Van Nostrand Reinhold
PULS, Herta *The Art of Cutwork and Appliqué* Batsford
SHORT, Eirian *Quilting: technique, design and application* Batsford
THOMAS, Mary *Mary Thomas's Embroidery Book* Hodder & Stoughton
WHYTE, Kathleen *Design in Embroidery* Batsford
WILSON, Jean *Weaving is Fun* Van Nostrand Reinhold

Embroidery is a magazine published by EG Enterprises for the Embroiderers' Guild and contains information on the latest books, exhibitions and sources of supply for a range of materials, as well as articles on contemporary and historical embroidery. It can be ordered from Apartment 41A, Hampton Court Palace, East Molesey, Surrey KT8 9AU.

Suppliers

Many basic fabrics can easily be bought from local shops, particularly those which sell Indian fabrics for saris. Markets are also a source of good inexpensive fabrics for backgrounds and curtain nets for free darning. Sometimes a fabric which has been washed and used for household purposes may be suitable for a particular design, and jumble sales have a wealth of such fabrics, including velvets shaded with wear, and crêpes.

Borovick Fabrics Ltd
16 Berwick Street
London W1V 4HP
Exotic, exciting fabrics including organzas, shot fabrics, satins and nets in irresistible colours. Well worth a visit

Felt and Hessian Shop
34 Grenville Street
London EC1
Felt and hessian

Iqbal Textiles
394–396 Stapleton Road
Bristol
Shot organzas, chiffons, satins, silks, etc.

John Lewis
Oxford Street
London W1
(Local branches have more limited but good selections.)
Many basic cottons, polyesters, etc., and household furnishing fabrics for backgrounds

*Livingstone Textile Co. Ltd
St Michael's Lane
Bridport
Dorset
A range of basic and patterned fabrics including calico, dyed cotton drill, polyester, etc., in large quantities

*MacCulloch and Wallis
25–26 Dering Street
London W1R 0BH
A variety of basic, traditional embroidery fabrics

*Mace and Nairn
89 Crane Street
Salisbury
Wiltshire
A good range of traditional embroidery fabrics

*Pongees Ltd
184–186 Old Street
London EC1V 9BP
Huge variety of plain silks, minimum order 25 metres

*Shades
57 Candlemas Lane
Deaconsfield
Bucks HP9 1AE
Specialist, hard-to-trace materials, including hot and cold water dissolve for machine lace, square nets, etc.

*60 Plus Textiles
Barley
Nelson
Lancs
Patchwork bales, shirting, sheeting, etc.

*Whaleys (Bradford) Ltd
Harris Court
Great Horton
Bradford
Hot and cold water dissolve materials. Wide range of basic and specialist fabrics including silk, cotton, wool, etc., in natural colours suitable for use as backgrounds for dyeing. A sample pack is to be recommended (payment required).

*George Weil & Sons Ltd
Riding House Street
London W1
Wide calico, silks, nun's veiling, etc.

* Mail order service available.

Index